THE

Reclaiming Your Worth

LIES

by Embracing

THAT

God's Truth

BIND

Tara Johnson

Guideposts

A Gift from Guideposts

Thank you for your purchase! We want to express our gratitude for your support with a special gift just for you.

Dive into ***Spirit Lifters***, a complimentary e-book that will fortify your faith, offering solace during challenging moments. Its 31 carefully selected scripture verses will soothe and uplift your soul.

Please use the QR code or go to **guideposts.org/spiritlifters** to download.

The Lies That Bind: Reclaiming Your Worth by Embracing God's Truth

Published by Guideposts
100 Reserve Rd., Suite E200
Danbury, CT 06810
Guideposts.org

Cover design by Faceout Studio, Addie Lutzo
Cover imagery from Shutterstock
Interior design by PerfecType, Inc.
Typeset by Aptara, Inc.

ISBN 978-1-965859-35-3 (softcover)
ISBN 978-1-965859-36-0 (epub)

Printed and bound in the United States of America
10 9 8 7 6 5 4 3 2 1

THE LIES THAT BIND

Contents

INTRODUCTION: The Lie about Me 1
CHAPTER 1: The Lie of Fear 13
CHAPTER 2: The Lie of Productivity 31
CHAPTER 3: The Lie of Perfectionism 45
CHAPTER 4: The Lie of People-Pleasing 61
CHAPTER 5: The Lie of Depression 77
CHAPTER 6: The Lie of Insecurity 97
CHAPTER 7: The Lie of Willpower 117
CONCLUSION: Reclaiming Our Worth 139

Appendix: Finding Truth in God's Word 145
Small-Group Guide 155
Notes 175
Acknowledgments 177
A Note from the Editors 179

INTRODUCTION
The Lie about Me

Sobs shook my chest as I lay face down in my dingy bathroom, my fingers clenching the burgundy threads of the bathmat beneath my shuddering body.

I couldn't breathe.

The pressure squeezed my chest like a vise as salt filled my mouth. With a guttural cry, I let the tears drip down my cheeks and off my chin. As the sobs eased, I flipped onto my back and stared up at the white popcorn ceiling overhead. I couldn't keep everyone happy. The demands on my time kept growing; each day was filled to the brim, and my nerves were frayed beyond repair. If I couldn't keep the plates spinning, I would disappoint everyone. And then what would I be? A failure. Rejected. Unloved. I was drowning in a spiral of emotions, and my self-worth was shredding in the process.

Perhaps I had never truly understood my worth to begin with.

God, this isn't the life You promised me. You said when I gave my heart to You, I would be flooded with joy, but all I feel is pain. I've poured out myself for others, but I have received so little in return.

Only exhaustion and an empty ache that chases me wherever I go. If this is all there is—living for approval and producing more and more only to grow emptier—then take me out of this chaos and let me die.

That was the night I learned to hate bathmats—and when I realized I had traded God's love for a lie.

Strange, isn't it? I find bathmats useful, much better than dropping a towel on the floor. I've seen beautiful ones and ugly ones, but I won't buy any of them. Every time I see one, I'm transported to the night I lay on the floor asking God to end my life.

How did I get to that point? I was Super Christian. I was a preacher's kid. I did whatever needed to be done in my church and family with a grin and a swish of my cape. I was always smiling, always volunteering, always available. But at some point, I lost my way. And I began to wonder if God's promises to me were lies.

I had fallen for a lie all right, but it wasn't that serving God and others was too hard. Somehow, slowly over time, I fell into a life of paralyzing fear, fueled by insecurity that drove me to think I had to do more, be more, to keep everyone around me happy. Perfectionism and people-pleasing became my drug. I clung to the misbelief that approval equals love, and it led me into the cold arms of depression—a suffering so heavy it nearly destroyed me.

THE UNIVERSAL PROBLEM

I stood before a group of female inmates at the Pine Bluff Women's Correctional Facility and wiped my sweaty hands down my jeans. I had spoken at prisons dozens of times, but working with the women was always harder than ministering to men. Male inmates, although often wary, were grateful for the opportunity to leave their cell. They smiled and listened and thanked me for coming with genuine humility. Not so the women. These ladies were tough. Hardened. Angry. Whatever I had to say, they weren't buying. I later learned this hard shell was usually a tough façade used to protect their crushed hearts and hopes. But at the time, all I could see was a sea of scowling faces.

I tried opening with jokes and stories but received no response. A bead of cold sweat ran down my back. After requesting they open their Bibles to Daniel 1, I asked them if they had ever fallen for a lie.

A frowning woman in the back spoke up. "What kind of lie?"

I paused. "Any kind, I suppose. How many of you have ever thought you were worthless?"

Every hand shot up, and my heart ached. Not surprising, considering where we were and the trauma that had led many of them to this moment.

A week later, I was teaching at a women's retreat at a local church. These women were smiling and laughing, talking about the latest clothing styles, whose children had started kindergarten, and where they wanted to go for summer vacation. When I asked these women if they had ever believed they were worthless, the smiles quickly vanished, and every person in the room timidly raised her hand.

I was floored. Of the 200 women I had spoken to in one week, every single one had once believed she was worthless. It couldn't be blamed on their socioeconomic status or whether they were single or married, young or old, incarcerated or free. It soon became apparent that we have all struggled with this issue or something similar.

I've talked to hundreds of women since then, gathering as much information as I could, asking, "What are the false things you have believed about yourself?" These are some of the most common answers:

"No one could ever love me if they knew the real me."

"If I feel something, it must be true."

"I don't have value."

"God couldn't love me after what I've done."

"I'm a horrible wife/mom/daughter/friend."

"My past will always destroy my future."

"God is against me."

"If my life circumstances were different, I would be different."

On and on the list goes. And in these statements, I see my own story.

THE DOORMAT

I really don't know how it began. I suppose I could blame genetics. Being high-strung runs in my family, but I believe there is more to it than that. As I mentioned before, I'm a preacher's kid (PK), and growing up in the church is interesting to say the least. You see the good, the bad, and the ugly in people. Often what church members say and what they do are two separate things, and when times get hard, it's easy to blame others. Human beings are really good at picking one another apart.

I never once felt pressure from my parents to act a certain way, say certain things, or keep up any kind of pretense to protect Dad's ministry. But somewhere along the way, I began to internalize the need to be agreeable. After all, there are dozens of verses about "keeping the peace" and striving for unity:

> *Make every effort to keep the unity of the Spirit through the bond of peace.* Ephesians 4:3, NIV

> *How good and pleasant it is when God's people live together in unity!* Psalm 133:1, NIV

> *I appeal to you, brothers and sisters, in the name of our Lord Jesus Christ, that all of you agree with one another in what you say and that there be no divisions among you, but that you be perfectly united in mind and thought.* 1 Corinthians 1:10, NIV

Armed with these verses—and hating to have anyone mad at me—I decided to do my all to please those around me. When the church needed a pianist, I dutifully took piano lessons, a skill which has served me well over the years and one I deeply enjoy. My first piano teacher was a woman who hailed from Japan and had only been in the states for a few months. I couldn't understand a word she said, except for her continual question, "You understand me, yes?" Instead of saying "no," I would nod and smile. Maybe if I smiled enough, she would stop asking.

I learned to sing solos at church when there was no one willing to do it and relished all the praise I received. The words of the deacons and sweet older women did something powerful to my heart. I was lauded and bragged on. I found my worth in what I could do.

As I grew into my teen years, I taught Vacation Bible School, led devotional time at church camp, and offered to help teachers in their Sunday school classes. I was the model preacher's kid, and I loved the attention that brought me.

And then I got married. My husband and I moved away, joined a new church, and I was faced with an obstacle: I needed to impress a brand-new group of people. No problem. All I had to do was smile and say yes to any request. If the pastor said the church windows needed to be washed at midnight, I dutifully appeared with Windex in hand.

Some folks call this behavior *people-pleasing*. I prefer the term *approval addiction*, but each term points to a bigger problem.

THE RODEO CLOWN

"Tara, why can't you look me in the eye?"

My friend's question sliced to the quick. We had been chatting for over forty minutes, and the topic had drifted from the mundane to more personal topics, which make me uncomfortable. When I know someone is peeling back layers and taking a peek underneath the mask of perfection and confidence I work so hard to keep fixed in place, the intensity of their stare is too much. I don't want them to see the trembling mess I am. So, I take a sudden interest in my shoes. Or the couch cushion. Or the coffee cup clutched in my fingers. Anything other than their probing stare.

Though I've made tremendous strides in the past few years—I'm learning to say no, to express my thoughts and opinions without worrying what others might think of me—I'm not exactly *dancing* in freedom. Still, God has been teaching me to *walk* in it, though some days it feels more like I'm tiptoeing around in His grace. That's OK. Imperfect progress and all that. But why do I still have trouble looking people in the eye? If eyes are windows to the soul, I try my best to keep my soul shuttered and locked away from view.

I made some silly comment in response to my friend's pointed observation. Something intended to make her laugh. A joke. It's what I do. She smiled, but she wasn't through.

"Do you know what you remind me of? One of those rodeo clowns."

I blinked. "What do you mean?"

She smiled kindly, but she didn't shy away from the truth. "You know what the original rodeo clowns were intended to do, right? They were meant to distract the crowd from the blood and gore that had just occurred between the bull and rider. They diverted attention away from the serious issues by entertaining. Cover the grotesque with a smile and a funny routine." She squeezed my hand. "And sometimes a bit of greasepaint."

How faithful are the words of a friend. It was difficult to hear, but my friend was completely correct. Though God is restoring my broken places each and every day, there is still a part of me that longs to hide. A fragment of my spirit that lives in shame. Shame never wants to flaunt itself, does it? It covers. It distracts. It deflects. As Jennifer Dukes Lee worded it in her book *Love Idol,* "Because we can't make any peace with ourselves, we try instead to *hide* ourselves."[1]

Hiding can take all kind of forms. It doesn't have to be the mousy little girl ducking behind her mane of hair and folded arms. Shame and insecurity can be buried in the homecoming queen or the public speaker or, yes, even a rodeo clown. Some of us only want to be seen if we will be perceived as perfect, and we either avert our gaze or apply the greasepaint because we know we're not.

It has taken me awhile to identify how and why my battle with these lies occurred, but the chat with my friend forced me to realize all my laughter and clowning was a distraction from the pain I carried inside. When we aren't forced to examine our hearts, we muddle through life with coping mechanisms designed to hide the real problem.

THE LIES

You may not have ever struggled with approval addiction like I did, but I'd wager we all struggle with *something*. Whether through our upbringing, poor decisions, or the destructive decisions of others, we have all been wounded. Shame, rejection, abandonment, death, abuse, betrayal, feeling unloved—all these have the power to usher in lies about our worth, our needs, or our place in this world.

Wounds can only be ignored for so long, and if they aren't dealt with, they can lead to a full-body infection. Our feeble attempts to ignore them or hide them from others may work in the short-term, but it doesn't get to the root of our pain. And it doesn't allow us to heal.

My own struggles are far from unique. After speaking to thousands of women in multiple states and across diverse situations, many of us have succumbed to the knee-wobbling lie of fear. Whether due to work stress or pressure to be the perfect wife, mother, daughter, or friend, we wrap up our worth in how well we perform. Many of us believe we have to have the perfect bodies, homes, and children to be loved. We crave acceptance, thinking it will fill the void inside. We compare ourselves to others and mark our worth not by our successes but by our failures. We battle dark depression and find our meager confidence wavering. Worse still, many of us believe we'll never truly be free of the anguish gnawing at our hearts.

These lies are often far sneakier than we give them credit for. Sometimes, our misbeliefs feel identical to truth. They *feel* right because at one moment in our life someone or some event reinforced them. As we grow up, those misbeliefs are clues we receive that tell us how the world seems to work. They shape our worldview and become the filter through which we see everything.

If I were to ask three different people to envision a barking dog and describe it to me, I might receive three different answers. Some folks might picture a cute little yapping puppy. Others may conjure images of their hyper chihuahua barking with abandon at a squirrel outside the window. People who have been attacked or frightened by a ferocious dog will likely picture a snapping German shepherd. Our past experiences shape the way we see the world.

The things we believe about ourselves become the motivating factor in how we behave, what we say, how we treat others—or let others treat us. It molds our perspective. I would daresay most of the bad decisions we make are rooted in a lie we've never confronted.

BUZZ LIGHTYEAR

We know that lies hurt us, but they are especially destructive when we believe them. Let me give you an example.

When my son, Nate, was four, I noticed the toilet in his bathroom kept getting clogged so badly my husband needed professional plumbing equipment to fix it. What he discovered was a handful of tiny green army men that had been flushed down the commode.

Hmm. The girls were too big to have done something so silly, so that left only one suspect: Nate.

When I asked him if he had flushed his toys down the toilet, his eyes grew wide, and he shook his head. "Uh-uh. Not me."

I pursed my lips and studied him. "Then who did it?"

He grinned, brown eyes twinkling with barely repressed mischief. "I think Buzz Lightyear did it."

Sure. Buzz Lightyear clogged our commode. I didn't believe him for a nanosecond, and he got in trouble for lying. His fib didn't hurt me because I didn't fall for his ridiculous attempt to wiggle free from the truth. If I had actually bought his story, I would be a neurotic mess, constantly peeking around every corner to make sure this invisible *Toy Story* troublemaker wasn't tormenting my family.

For a more practical example, I often think of one of my dearest friends. She is a poet, excels in her workplace, and is a martial arts expert. Her earliest memories are of her parents telling her they didn't want her. Sadly, she believed them. The result was years of battling depression, pornography addiction, and self-harm.

Lies usually confirm our deepest fear and have the power, if we let them, to strip away the freedom Jesus died to give us. Lies leave us in chains—physically, emotionally, and spiritually. They bind us and keep us stuck, propelling us to strive for more but denying us freedom.

In *Present Over Perfect*, Shauna Niequist states, "Years ago, a wise friend told me that no one ever changes until the pain level gets high enough.... The inciting incident for life change is almost always heartbreak—something becomes broken beyond repair, too heavy to carry; in the words of the recovery movement, unmanageable."[2] When our discomfort becomes too great to ignore, that is the moment when we realize something has to change.

To put it another way, many of us are thirsty, but we cannot find the water to quench our parched souls, in part because we're looking for satisfaction in things that cannot satisfy. What each of our battered hearts longs for is Jesus, yet it's difficult for us to recognize the Way, the Truth, and the Life when our souls have fallen for a false alternative. In the Gospel of John, Jesus tells us this: "Let anyone who is thirsty come to me and drink. Whoever believes in me, as Scripture has said, rivers of living water will flow from within them" (John 7:37–38, NIV).

There is a direct correlation between our willingness to face our broken places and our ability to be free. If you're craving peace, joy, and freedom and don't know how to find it, this book is for you.

EXPOSING THE LIES

The following chapters explore the lies many of us have believed. These lies are created by fear, productivity, perfectionism, people-pleasing, depression, insecurity, and willpower. We will dive deep into discovering how these lies begin, what they promise, and the result from their presence in our lives. More importantly, we will unearth how to expose them to the light of God's love.

I ask you to prayerfully consider my own experiences with these lies and ask yourself if there are similarities between my story and your own. How do you currently feel in your journey? Are you exhausted? Overjoyed? Peaceful? Scattered? Hurting? Pretending? Ask God to show you what He would like you to know as we scrutinize each lie and dig to the root of their origins.

I pray you will learn how to identify your wounds, expose the lies you might have believed, and embrace your worth in Christ. Knowing who we belong to changes our perspectives and, ultimately, our futures.

If you're exhausted, tired from battling the same old storms and the same old patterns, there is hope. Your current circumstances don't have to become your destiny. Let's explore together.

BIBLE VERSE

Dear friends, do not believe every spirit, but test the spirits to see whether they are from God. (1 John 4:1, NIV)

READER TAKEAWAY

At one time or another, we have all fallen for a lie, and believing that lie will leave us stuck in an exhausting cycle.

THE TRUTH

Lies have the power to wreak havoc in every aspect of our lives, but our current struggle doesn't have to be the conclusion of our story.

QUESTION

What lie have you believed about yourself?

CHAPTER 1

The Lie of Fear

When my daughter, Bethany, and her boyfriend, Dylan, now my son-in-law, were in high school, they didn't have a car and begged me to take them to see a scary movie—a *very* scary movie. According to my daughter, this was the kind of scary movie that teenagers around the globe excitedly watched with bated breath, their fingers trembling as they dug into tubs of buttery popcorn.

I'm not a fan of creepy flicks because, well, they're horrifying. But despite my usual avoidance of things that cause pain and lack of sleep, I agreed to their request with a smile because, although I'm not a fan of horror, there is one aspect I enjoy: frightening the people who go with me.

I confess, I was more than amused at the shrieking teens as they startled at the jump scares that peppered the movie. Popcorn flew. Girls screamed. I didn't even pay attention to the story. I was too busy studying the terrified kids who huddled in groups, peering through their fingers at the screen.

On our way home, Bethany turned on every light in the car. "That was crazy. I'm not going to sleep for a week."

Dylan shook his head. "I don't normally get scared, but that was rough. When I get home, I'm going to go to my room and put a stack of Bibles in front of the door before I crawl into bed."

I laughed at their melodrama and saw a once-in-a-lifetime opportunity as we drove down the long, curvy road to Dylan's family's home. No security lights. No businesses. Just a winding stretch of country backroad.

After I dropped Dylan off, he trudged down the dark driveway to his front door when my itch to cause mischief grew too great to ignore. Rolling down the driver's side window, I yelled, "Run, Dylan! Run!"

I had no idea a big, tough football player could run that fast.

Bethany and I burst into laughter, and I received a text moments later.

Not cool, man. Not cool.

That's what fear does. It looks for an opportunity to yank the proverbial rug from beneath our feet. Fear delights when we flounder. It takes joy in watching our faith wobble like Jell-O. It's a sneaky, cold trickster, and it attacks far more often than we realize. It's something people across the globe experience daily.

Some fear is healthy. We fear getting hit by a car, so we look both ways before crossing a busy road. We fear getting burned, so we keep our hands away from a hot stove. We fear being abused by manipulators, so we keep tight boundaries around our personal lives. Not all fear is bad. Our brains constantly scan our environment for potential threats. It's built into our bodies as a God-given source of protection. The problem is our emotions often listen to fear's lies as a way of coping with life, even when we are not in physical danger. We let our minds flip through a thousand what-ifs that will likely never happen, ignoring the destruction fear creates around and inside us.

RUNNING TO SAFETY

When children are scared, whether it's from the proverbial monsters hiding under their beds, a strange noise they can't identify, the dark, or a thousand other terrifying scenarios, what do they usually do? Most cry out for their mom or dad. But it's not enough to explain that "monsters don't exist" or "the noise is just the air conditioner." They long for comfort from the ones they trust. They want to be seen, heard, and comforted. Good parents scoop up their children and wrap them in their arms, shushing them with sweet words and gentle lullabies.

When my oldest daughter was a small child, she insisted that after our nightly bedtime story and prayer, her daddy needed to stand watch in the hallway. After all, monsters might be lurking. She would insist that she knew monsters weren't real, but having someone stand guard let her relax. So my dutiful husband would heroically patrol the hallway, his marching as practiced as a Marine. Every few minutes, he would softly chant, "One, two, three, four, no monster is getting near Bethany's door." Knowing he was there, dutifully keeping watch, allowed her little body to slip into slumber.

The story is sweet and silly and endearing, but it points to something vital for each of us to understand. First, even when we know our fears are unfounded, they *feel* real. And second, when we're scared, we crave the presence of the one we trust most.

The lie of fear says, "If I feel or think something, it must be true." It preys on our emotions. It tells us something is real, and, if we listen to it, we have knee-jerk reactions that often lead to disastrous results. In truth, most of what we fear doesn't come to pass. Instead, it robs us of the joy of the present, leaving an ominous cloud hanging over each part of our lives.

Those closest to Jesus felt this bone-rattling fear too.

> *As evening came, Jesus said to his disciples, "Let's cross to the other side of the lake." So they took Jesus in the boat and started out, leaving the crowds behind (although other boats followed). But soon a fierce storm came up. High waves were breaking into the boat, and it began to fill with water. Jesus was sleeping at the back of the boat with his head on a cushion. The disciples woke him up, shouting, "Teacher, don't you care that we're going to drown?" When Jesus woke up, he rebuked the wind and said to the waves, "Silence! Be still!" Suddenly the wind stopped, and there was a great calm. Then he asked them, "Why are you afraid? Do you still have no faith?" The disciples were absolutely terrified. "Who is this man?" they asked each other. "Even the wind and waves obey him!"* Mark 4:35–41, NLT

I've read this passage dozens of times, but not long ago, a simple phrase jumped out at me that I'd never noticed before. "Teacher, *don't you care* that we're going to drown?"

Don't you care? It's not that we don't expect life to throw us some curve balls. The pain hits when we assume God doesn't care about what is tormenting us, that He's allowing the bad things to happen. Then, when our thoughts spiral, we become consumed with panic-filled questions.

Don't You care that I can't break this addiction?
Don't You care that my marriage is falling apart?
Don't You care that my children are rebelling?

Don't You care that my bank account is empty?
Don't You care that my health is failing?
Don't You care that I long for children and have none?
Don't You care that everyone leaves me?
Don't You care that I feel unloved?

These kinds of thoughts leave us reeling, feeling like victims in a hopeless situation, playing exactly into the very goal of fear: to leave us stripped of the power God has given us.

Speaking for myself, bad choices are always the result when I choose to believe fear's lies. I try to coerce and manipulate, plan and scheme to get the outcome to align with my personal comfort, but I fail. Always. I've learned the wind and the waves don't obey my voice, but they do obey the voice of Jesus.

THE LIE OF FEAR: "FALSE EVIDENCE THAT APPEARS REAL"

One sunny June afternoon, I climbed on the lawn tractor to chop down the rapidly growing grass surrounding our home. My young son watched from our front porch, frowning and quickly becoming upset. The tractor was loud, and I figured he didn't like the noise it was making. Oh, but his concern stemmed from so much more.

Over the clatter of the tractor, I heard high-pitched squeals of laughter. My two girls were doubled over with giggles. What was so funny? I glanced behind me to see my three-year-old son running toward the moving tractor as fast as his chubby little legs could carry him. His face was puckered into a scowl. He held a broom in his hand and was charging at the metal monster, a look of death and determination in his eyes.

Think *Braveheart*, if you will.

The little stinker was preparing to attack the mower with a broom. I had to gas it all over the yard to escape him. It suddenly hit me what the problem was: he thought the big metal monster was trying to take away his mom.

I burst out laughing until rocks started raining down on me. My little hero was chucking stones as fast as he could, desperate to defend his poor mother.

Needless to say, that was my most adventurous mowing experience to date.

It must have been confusing to see a noisy, thundering metal monster whisk his mother away. Even more baffling was the way the vibrating beast kept circling the yard, refusing to spit his mommy out. So, my son had done what any valiant soldier would do—attack.

I thought the whole thing was pretty cute until those rocks started hitting me.

What seemed like a charming anecdote from an adult's point of view was terrifying from a child's perspective. Nate reacted out of fear. The assumption he made was the same one each of us makes, often on a daily basis. We lash out with knee-jerk reactions based on partial information and false assumptions.

Put another way, we live and make our choices based on false evidence that appears real—or FEAR for short.

Poor fellow. From his knowledge of the world and his childish experience, the tractor was loud, noisy, and scary. Even worse, this metal beast stole his mommy away. Surely, she was in danger. Surely something terrible was going to happen. Anything that loud *must* be dangerous.

But he was wrong.

He didn't know what I knew. What he saw as a disaster, I knew was a necessity. What he thought was dangerous was actually much safer than letting the grass grow, allowing snakes to infest the yard. I could see the big picture. He only understood a tiny portion of it.

When our circumstances threaten to overwhelm us, when are shaking in fear, when we let our emotions spiral into negativity and what-ifs, we need to remember that we only see a tiny part of God's plan. He is writing our stories. We shouldn't assume we know the ending based on the problems of page one.

My tractor-fighting son nearly hurt himself running at the mower with that broom. If I hadn't zoomed out of his reach, he would have thrust his weapon into that running mower, and, well, I shudder to think of the outcome. When we live in fear, when we have knee-jerk reactions based on partial information, overactive imaginations, or our ricocheting emotions, we end up doing a lot of damage to ourselves, to others, and especially to our walk with God. The peace of God cannot dwell with fear. The two are polar opposites.

Fear is normal. It's real, but we can't allow ourselves to wallow in its cold grip. Sometimes, it's nothing more than false evidence that appears real.

THE MASKS OF FEAR

I used to think fear was a nail-biting, knee-knocking kind of reaction to anything that seemed threatening. But it's much worse than that. Fear wears many masks, making itself look harmless. But fear is our enemy, and a smart enemy doesn't announce its attack before it strikes.

Part of the reason we struggle so much against fear is because it often is disguised as something completely different. The pompous, bombastic leader often overcompensates for his insecurities by incessant bragging. The gentle soul fearing vulnerability will often wear a mask with a hard veneer to keep love away and their heart safe. The mom who volunteers for every committee and church activity is often afraid her worth will decrease if she underperforms. Fear can disguise itself as anger because that emotion is easier to swim in than grief. The has-it-all-together wife with the perfect house and perfect life grasps for control because she dreads the pain she will feel when the illusion crumbles. In short, if fear is left unchecked, it bleeds into every area of our lives.

Fear sometimes avoids overt attacks but creeps in through physical sensations and odd behavior choices. Our stomachs cramp when our expectations aren't met or when we assume we've disappointed our loved ones. The foundation beneath our feet shifts, leaving us feeling vulnerable and exposed when someone we trust lets us down. Depression and exhaustion lurk from juggling so many responsibilities because we've been trying to keep people happy, not realizing that what we really fear is rejection. For some, failing is our greatest fear—something too horrific to endure—so we never let our house be messy, we refuse to get less than an A in school, we won't go out the door without wearing makeup, and we never dream or take risks.

The other faces of fear include procrastination, isolation, laziness, greed, addictions, excessive use of technology, busyness, and distraction. All these and more reveal the destructive work of anxiety clawing at our hearts.

Fear is much more than the mousy girl hiding behind her hair. It can drive the president of the bank, the cheerleader, or the person who appears to have everything. Über-confident people can be chased by the wildest of demons. How many lives have been destroyed because of fear? How many marriages ruined, how many children scarred, how many dreams unfulfilled, and how many people chained in the terrifying prison of addiction because of fear?

Graveyards are interesting places. I confess I have a fascination with them. For a writer, there is so much to be imagined in that dash between a headstone's birth date and death date. Most of us want to use that slip of time, our dashes, well. When I pass a cemetery, I can't help but wonder how many of the souls buried in its sod died with their dreams still inside them. How many were shackled by timidity? How many were held back by believing the naysayers and critics? How many quaked at the thought of being honest about who they really were?

For too many people, dreams were never achieved, never reached for, because they were too busy running from their fears.

So many of us are experiencing a half-lived life. We cower in the shadows, afraid to confront the wounds we need to expose to God's light. Fear says people could never love us and God could never forgive us if they knew who we really are. It keeps us trapped in cycles of people-pleasing, perfectionism, anxiety, and hypocrisy. Fear causes us to smile to camouflage our sadness, laugh to distract from our thoughts, and self-medicate to numb ourselves from our terror.

It steals our peace of mind, rattles our faith, and launches our emotions on a continually swinging pendulum. It suffocates. It breathes against the window of our hearts like a panting monster. It beats a refrain of "What if?" and taunts us with the perpetual thought that God isn't there. Left unchecked, it gives birth to a slew of other lies that have the potential to upend our lives.

Fear is a lie, and it's time to expose it to the light of truth.

LOVE OR FEAR?

I recently ran across a beautiful Cherokee story told by Briana Kennedy LaGrow that illustrates the struggle inside us perfectly.

In this story, a grandfather is teaching his grandson about life, telling him about two "wolves" that battle inside all of us.

> *"One [wolf] is evil. It is anger, envy, jealousy, sorrow, regret, greed, arrogance, self-pity, guilt, resentment, inferiority, lies, false pride, superiority, and ego. The other is good. It is joy, peace, love, hope, serenity, humility, kindness, benevolence, empathy, generosity, truth, compassion, and faith."*
>
> *The grandson thought about it for a minute and then asked his grandfather: "Which wolf wins?"*
>
> *The old [man] simply replied, "The one that you feed."*[3]

We have two natures inside. One is spiritual, and the other is carnal. The former is eternal, and the latter is temporal. The spiritual man is fueled by God's love, and the carnal is driven by angst and the desire to protect self. Love versus fear.

Love empowers, creates, helps us grow, and strengthens relationships. As 1 Corinthians 13 reminds us, love is patient, kind, not jealous or boastful. It doesn't need to puff up egos, nor does it dishonor others. It's not selfish but seeks the good in others. It doesn't think about all the ways it has been wronged, but it celebrates truth.

Fear is love's polar opposite. Fear is rooted in survival instincts and looking out for self-preservation. It's rash and judgmental, harsh and angry. It gossips and is marked by cruelty and pride. Fear fuels all the dark emotions that rattle our faith, and bad decisions are always the result.

One of my favorite verses is Isaiah 41:10 (NKJV): "Fear not, for I am with you; be not dismayed, for I am your God. I will strengthen you, yes, I will help you, I will uphold you with my righteous right hand." God encourages His children over and over again not to be afraid. Why? Well, one reason is because He knows every decision we make flows from either fear or love because love and fear cannot coexist. "There is no fear in love. But perfect love drives out fear, because fear has to do with punishment. The one who fears is not made perfect in love" (1 John 4:18, NIV).

PERFECT LOVE

To be honest, I've struggled with 1 John 4:18 for years. To get rid of fear, I need perfect love. Got it. But what does that mean? When I'm faced with a scary diagnosis, the bills that keep piling up, rebellious loved ones, and situations I can no longer control, that's when I realize I have no idea what to do. I feel powerless.

I know the Greek word for *drives* or *casts* (as in "perfect love *drives* out fear") has to do with a violent displacement. It means love grabs fear and throws it through the window. Descriptive. But what exactly is "perfect love"? How can I experience it?

After a teary therapy appointment for my son, God revealed the beauty of this phrase to me in a tender way. I had just left my son's elementary school after a difficult discussion. His therapists had explained that they knew something was going on with my joyful little firecracker but were unable to pinpoint the source of his issues. While sitting in a child-sized chair, my knees bumping the low table, I heard the words I had dreaded: "It might be time to test for autism."

Though I agreed in the moment, once my son and I were in the car, pulling out of the school's parking lot, I was overcome with an onslaught of what-ifs. What if my son battled a life of perpetual pain? What if he was rejected by his peers? What if he were bullied for being different? On and on the thoughts tumbled until the icy tentacles squeezing my heart grabbed me by the throat.

"Monny, sing Jee-Jee!"

My son could speak very few words, but there were three I always understood. *Monny* for *Mommy*, *sing*, and *Jee-Jee* for *Jesus*.

I blinked away the tears blurring my eyes. Peering into the rearview mirror, I saw my son's sunny smile and heard his sweet voice. "Jee-Jee love me. Jee-Jee mine. Jee-Jee love me. Jee-Jee mine…"

I sucked in a breath. Here I was, worrying over things I had no control over, and the source of my angst was lifting up praises to Jesus. I pushed down the stinging tears and smiled. "Good idea, buddy. Let's praise Jesus."

We sang song after song on the car ride home. With each melody, my fear evaporated. Why? Because fear dissolves in the presence of praise. The source of our praise, the One we worship is Jesus Christ. Fear cannot exist in His presence. It scatters like darkness shattered by light. Revelation twisted my heart with a surge of joy.

What does the Bible tell us about Jesus? It says repeatedly He is love. Perfect love.

Perfect love casts out fear.

Finally, I understood.

Perfect love is Jesus, God wrapped in human flesh. Perfect love goes to any length to save and any height to reach. Perfect love calls the prisoner his brother, redeems him, and sets him free.

Perfect love is complete, all consuming, with no traces of doubt in the power of the Holy One. Perfect love sets a glittering crown on the head of the orphan and calls her "Beloved Daughter."

Fear has no chance against such a love.

FEAR BUSTERS

In addition to praise, there are other ways to dismantle fear. Some of them are simple, like flooding our minds with Bible verses about God's promises to His children or carefully choosing what we watch, listen to, or absorb. What we consume affects our bodies, our emotions, and our spirits.

I'm a certified body language expert and while completing my certification, I was surprised to learn that all body language comes from the limbic system—the part of the brain responsible for freeze, fight, or flight responses. In short, all our wiring for body language is intrinsically linked to our brain's hypervigilance in continually scanning for threats.

Being afraid of harmful things like fire, poison, dangerous creatures, and criminals is important and necessary. The problem comes when our fears eclipse our view of God and His ability to keep us safe. Why is it easier to trust Him with our eternity than the daily activities of our lives?

Worse still, we often don't understand how much God values us, so we look over our shoulder, waiting for harm to swoop in, even though He has told us repeatedly that He will never leave us. He guides us through the darkest valleys, holding our hands when we tremble, and carrying us when our quaking knees give way.

Ultimately, fear misplaces our focus. It's vital that we measure the size of our fear against the size of our God. When we give in to the terror fear produces, we aren't focusing on who God is. We become consumed with self and survival and rely on our own feeble attempts to chase it away instead of trusting in God, His Word, and His character.

FEAR VERSUS ANXIETY

I want to pause here and say that the lie of fear differs from a clinical diagnosis of an anxiety disorder. Much harm has been done by well-meaning people to those suffering with debilitating anxiety. Some believe if they share the perfect scripture or say the perfect prayer, the anxious will be able to break free. If only it were that simple.

Some have even suggested anxiety is a lack of faith. I heartily disagree.

Chemical imbalances and neurological disorders are part of living in a broken world with broken bodies. If we take medication for heart function, inject insulin for diabetes, or wear glasses for weak eyesight, then we can treat our other organs with medications that help them work properly. May we never wield the Word of God as a weapon against the hurting.

WHISTLING ON THE LEDGE

Not long ago, I attended a beautiful writer's retreat in Monterey, California. Something interesting happened during the final afternoon session. While craving a breath of fresh ocean air, I stepped outside and peered over the hotel's third-floor balcony that jutted out over rocky crags below. Looking down, my heart slammed against my ribs. On the second floor, I could see a window washer, standing atop a six-foot ladder perched on the edge of a narrow walkway. An extremely narrow walkway. Stranger still, he was joyfully whistling as he attended to his tasks. There was absolutely no ledge to keep his ladder from sliding to the rocks below. None.

I watched him in fascination for several long minutes. Every time he moved farther down the walkway, swinging that ladder wide over the air, dangling the metal contraption into space, my stomach clenched. But the man's step never wavered. His whistling never ceased. If anything, it was like the task was second nature to him, no different than breathing or eating. If it were me wobbling on that ledge, then the scene wouldn't have been nearly so tranquil. I wouldn't be whistling—I'd be shrieking. And that's just me getting to the top of a ladder, the second-story ledge not included.

The window washer was comfortable because he had done this task so many times that fear was no longer a factor. He knew the ledge. He knew its strength and its width. He'd tested it over and over again. He could move in freedom with a song on his lips while an ocean raged behind him and sharp rocks sat like teeth underneath because he had faith the ledge would hold him up. And it did.

It's the same with God. The older I grow, the easier it's becoming to trust Him. Why? Because He's proved Himself faithful over and over again. The storms are just as strong, the fire just as hot, the emotions just as loud, but the fear doesn't rattle me as it once did. Oh, there's still some fear. But my faith is stronger, a wee bit closer to becoming unshakable.

The deeper we move and live in the knowledge of God's love for us, the more the fear shrinks. Maybe someday I'll even be able to whistle atop a ladder perched on a second-story ledge.

UNTANGLING THE CORDS OF FEAR

Second Corinthians 10:5 (NIV) declares, "We demolish arguments and every pretension that sets itself up against the knowledge of God, and we take captive every thought to make it obedient to Christ." To crush fear, we have to know who holds our future in His hands. We praise Him and let His perfect love take hold. Then, we take our thoughts and worries captive. We strangle those "Don't you cares" and "What-ifs" and replace them with the words of the great I AM.

Instead of letting our minds shout our fears over and over in a loop, we capture our thoughts by naming our emotions. *I am feeling _______________ because I'm afraid of _______________.* Then, after stating our fear, we remind ourselves that our emotions aren't necessarily the same as our current situation. *"I'm afraid I'm going to fail, but that has not happened yet."* Follow that truthful statement with a reminder of God's promises. *"Jesus said He will never leave me nor forsake me. No matter what comes, He will be by my side."* Living in this broken world, we are not guaranteed a trauma-free life, but God did promise to carry us through every storm. Finish those thoughts by praising Him for who He is and what He has done. Feed love and starve fear.

Speaking for myself, it wasn't until I let Him pull the mask of fear away that I realized I had been hiding in plain sight for years. We may think masks protect us, but what they really do is hide our identity. We were created for confidence and freedom. We were designed to make choices rooted in joy and love, not rash decisions reached in alarm. God wants His children to be the most secure people on earth. He doesn't want us to tiptoe around, *hoping* we have value; instead, He yearns for us to walk *knowing* we have worth. We were made to dance in freedom, not cower in fear.

These days, I refuse to live in the land of what-ifs when my God is I AM.

BIBLE VERSE

There is no fear in love. But perfect love drives out fear, because fear has to do with punishment. The one who fears is not made perfect in love. (1 John 4:18, NIV)

READER TAKEAWAY

If any of us is struggling with feeling our life is no longer joyful, then it may be because we are living with some form of unidentified fear.

THE TRUTH

God is greater than our fear. By turning to Him and letting Him expose it, we begin the process of healing.

QUESTIONS

What are some of the masks you wear to hide your fear? How do you think those masks protect you? In what ways are they actually allowing you to avoid the problem and alienating you from true peace?

CHAPTER 2

The Lie of Productivity

It had been a long day. I'd made my way to the gym before the sun rose, driven one coughing child to the doctor, homeschooled another one, dashed to the grocery store, fixed three meals for my family, and spent four hours in my office trying to catch up on writing work. I was tired but duty had called again and again. As I dragged my weary feet to the laundry room, I tossed the load of damp clothes into the dryer and slammed the door with a rattling bang. After hitting the button to start the cycle, I trudged to bed and blissfully passed out.

The next morning, I reached into the dryer to retrieve our clothes and grimaced. *Ugh. Still wet*, I thought. *Well, I had been tired the night before. Maybe I hadn't started the dryer after all.* This time I made sure to hit the big, round button. It sprang to life and hummed with activity.

An hour passed, and still the dryer ran. Then another hour and another. Frowning, I made my way to the dryer and opened it. The clothes had been tumbling all morning, but they were just as wet as they'd been the night before.

My trusty dryer was broken. It had been spinning for hours but there was no heat—working hard but going nowhere and doing nothing.

How often do I do the same thing?

MERIT BADGES

Our world is programmed to reward productivity. Boy and Girl Scouts receive merit badges. Schools award certificates of achievement for making the honor roll. Athletes receive varsity jackets and medals for sports. Employers grant promotions and financial bonuses to employees as they climb the corporate ladder. Back in the day, churches even rewarded the faithful with Sunday school pins.

Not long ago, I signed up to run a Thanksgiving week 5K race with friends. As we chatted about how many of us were likely to walk—or rather gasp—our way across the finish line, one of my friends said, "Do we get a T-shirt? A medal or ribbon for participating?"

I shrugged. "I have no idea. Why?"

My friend scowled. "What's the point of doing it unless I receive some kind of award for putting out all that effort?"

The question stopped me for a moment. What *was* the point? I suppose it depends on the person and their motivation. The thought of receiving an "atta-girl" never even crossed my mind. I just wanted to spend time with my buddies while doing something active. Nothing more. But those striving for external rewards may find that productivity and accomplishment can be a slippery slope.

I know because I've lived it, and I have no desire to return.

Sometimes I wonder if we're wrapped in so many ribbons, medals, diplomas, and trophies, we can't see how much of our life is geared toward achieving the very things that pull us away from intimacy with our Creator.

TOXIC PRODUCTIVITY

How many of us have bought into the myth of multitasking? We can easily fix dinner while listening to an audiobook and also helping our child with homework as we fold socks, all at the same time. Work harder, work *smarter*, and get more accomplished each day.

The problem is people across the globe are now less content, more stressed out, and more distracted than any other time in history. What we're actually doing when we multitask is forcing our brains to switch back and forth between the multiple tasks that need our attention. We aren't doing a lot of things well. In fact, we're doing many tasks poorly—and our minds and hearts are getting scrambled in the process.

There's now a new phenomenon being coined in the business world: *toxic productivity*. This refers to people who prioritize constant work and output at the expense of their own mental and physical well-being. I would add spiritual well-being too. This leads to chronic stress, burnout, and failing health.

It would be easy to blame this problem on our culture's obsession with perfectionism or how social media encourages competition between all our friends and our highlight reels. However, I believe the problem is rooted much deeper than mere social phenomenon.

So how has toxic productivity been created?

I believe the problem begins in each individual heart. I'll start with my own.

TO DO OR TO BE?

Why do I struggle so much with the insatiable need *to do*? *To fix*? *To accomplish*? I know I'm not the only one. Our world is filled with people who earn degree after degree yet never get any wiser. Who climb the ladder of success yet find no satisfaction for the gaping hole inside. Even more dangerous, many Christians shroud the god of busyness in the cloak of "doing the Lord's work" or going about "their calling," never realizing they are trying to fill a broken cistern. They use the name of God as a cover, as a way to fill their own need for self-importance. We have tied our self-worth to our achievements.

I'm a list maker. I enjoy the rush of dopamine that fills my brain every time I check another item off my to-do list. It's accomplishment. A goal achieved. A sign I'm doing something. Though there's nothing wrong with creating a to-do list for ourselves, too many Christians—myself included—have viewed our relationship with God as a checklist. We take time to pray because we're supposed to. We read the Bible because it is required. We ask God to use us to do great things for Him because it's on our spiritual to-do list. "Change the world." Check.

Please don't get me wrong. I'm not saying we're supposed to be lazy and apathetic. Far from it. Jesus said blessed is the one who, when He returns, is found doing (Matthew 24:46). We need be busy with our Father's business. But I fear that for too many of us, *accomplishing for God* has replaced *having a relationship with God* as priority number one. Before we dig in deeper, let me pause for a moment to say that achievement in and of itself is not wrong. Whatever we do should be done with excellence and for the glory of God (1 Corinthians 10:31). Nor is it wrong to receive an accolade from time to time. The problem is when we tie our identity to our accomplishments.

DEPENDING ON ME

Sometimes I think we humans give ourselves far too much credit.

We think the world will collapse without us. We are irreplaceable. The universe begins with our birth and ends with our death. We have a mountain of tasks that depend on our follow-through. Our own self-importance is staggering—or it can be, if we actually believe all this to be the truth.

I especially find my propensity to think I'm more important than I am in my pesky moments of indecisiveness. I usually don't rush into making a decision because I'm terrified I might make one shaky move outside of God's will. One tiptoe past the invisible line in the sand will spiral me into a life of doom. I'll never forget what a friend told me when I shared my angst with him one day. He grinned. "So, you think you'll do something, especially in ignorance, that God is unable to fix? Sorry, but you're not that powerful."

Good point.

So if I'm not big enough to topple the God of the universe, why do I keep striving, acting like the world and all its spinning plates are dependent on me? Why am I perpetually on a hamster wheel trying to do more, be more? Why am I so focused on *doing* instead of *being*?

Somewhere along the way, I fell for the lie of productivity that screams, "If I produce good results, I have worth."

CREATED FOR MORE

When God created the world, He spoke it into existence and called out what each element would birth and how each particle of creation was meant to function.

> *Then God said, "Let the land sprout with vegetation—every sort of seed-bearing plant, and trees that grow seed-bearing fruit. These seeds will then produce the kinds of plants and trees from which they came." … Then God said, "Let the waters swarm with fish and other life. Let the skies be filled with birds of every kind."* Genesis 1:11, 20, NLT

Waters gave nourishment and life to fish. Air was intended for birds. Out of the soil, trees, flowers, and fruit grew. But notice how things changed when God created humans.

> *Then God said, "Let us make human beings in our image."* Genesis 1:26, NLT

Life begot life. Fish thrive in water, apple trees in soil, and we, my friend, were designed to thrive on connection with God. Yet ever since the dawn of the world, we have tried to replace that bond with other things.

Degrees, promotions, accomplishments, accolades, fame—the list goes on and on. We try to fill the emptiness inside by having more, acquiring more, doing more, but, just like a fish gasping for air outside of water, we find ourselves exhausted, resentful, angry, and, yes, dying.

Not long ago, our family watched the old Disney movie *Cool Runnings*. John Candy's character said something quite profound. "Derice, a gold medal is a wonderful thing. But if you're not enough without it, you'll never be enough with it."[4] This thought lingered for days. We are more than what we produce. Productivity is an idol, promising *feelings* of worth but ultimately giving exhaustion, franticness, and heavy loads to bear.

As you'll see in the coming chapters, I filled my own emptiness with people-pleasing and perfectionism, but both are moving targets that never offered lasting satisfaction. For some, their mind and emotions are stuck on replay, repeating oft-used mantras until they're weary. *I should want to give my time and energy. I should help more. I should be a better mom, a better wife. Give more. Do more. Should, should, should. Do. Do. Do.*

The problem with those *shoulds* is that they fill us with guilt for some kind of perceived failure. They leave us burned out, weary, hopeless, and open for spiritual manipulation. *Shoulds* require us to do more and more to keep up. Why? Because we have become addicted to the false high we receive from accolades. Ministry is replaced with applause. We crave visibility because being seen makes us feel valuable.

When we live without knowing our true worth, we swap peace and freedom for shackles of exhaustion.

WHO AM I IF I'M NOT ACHIEVING?

Identity never hinges on what we do. It is unconditionally based on who we are. If the foundation of our identity isn't secure as a child of God, it is likely an identity tied to an addiction or wound. Whether we realize it or not, our entire life has revolved around our longing for God. We continually try to find contentment in other things when He is the only source that will ever satisfy.

With God, the priority is always presence over performance, intimacy over independence. Moses so desired God's presence that he refused to lead the Israelites without Him. The wise prophet told God he'd rather call the entire trip off than do it alone (Exodus 33). Imagine if we took the same approach, not entering into any project or adventure without God—not out of obligation or duty, but simply because we crave His presence more than our plans?

God doesn't really need us to do things for Him. He's self-sustaining. He spoke the world into existence. He hung the stars and calls each one by name. He saw us in our mothers' wombs and knew every aspect of our thoughts and emotions and who we would be before we were even born. We can't really impress Him with a stack of degrees and achievements. Instead of doing things *for* God, He invites us to rest and *know* Him. And as we sit in His presence, we learn who we are in Him.

What I can achieve means very little in comparison to what I believe about myself. I can work with high output, like a conveyor belt in a factory, but what I produce is external. Who and what I truly am is internal. Worth comes from the inside out. Not the other way around. And who I am inside is based on God's love—a love so deep that it doesn't depend on either my greatest achievements or my worst mistakes.

THE SOCCER BALL

Imagine that you've purchased a soccer ball for your six-year-old child. You can't wait to surprise them. You can picture the delight on their face when they hold it in their arms. You bring it home and hold it behind your back, waiting for just the right moment to pull out the surprise.

"Hey, kiddo. I got you something today."

Their eyes light up. "You did? What is it? Can I have it?"

You laugh and pull it from behind your back. "Here you go."

Two big dimples pop appear in their cheeks as they grin and clutch the new treasure. "A soccer ball! I can't wait to play with it!"

You kneel in front of them, your face serious. "This soccer ball is important. I got it for you so you'll practice. You need to practice all the time so you can play high school soccer and get a scholarship to attend a good college. Your whole future is riding on this. Then I expect you to play professionally someday, go all the way to the World Cup and score the winning goal for your team. You got that, kiddo?"

"Huh?"

This scenario is laughable. Nobody in their right mind buys a soccer ball for their six-year-old with the sole purpose of trying to mold them into a World Cup champion. No. You buy your child a soccer ball because you want to play with them. You want to spend time with them. It's about laughing together, playing together. Being in the moment. Making memories.

And that's what God wants too.

He doesn't want your checklist. He doesn't need you to accomplish anything for Him. He's got it covered. When the time is right, He allows us to partner with Him so we can see the jaw-dropping things He can do—not because He needs us but because it teaches *us* how awesome *He* is. It doesn't build His faith in us but our faith in Him.

God is inviting us to know Him as a good, perfect Father. Put down the checklists. Set aside the need to *do* in order to fill your own worth inside. He died for you and has already declared you were worth His sacrifice. He wants you to know Him. He has so much to share, so much love to lavish on you.

CHECKLISTS

For the high achievers out there, there is one sure way to tell if you're struggling with the lie of productivity. Look at your to-do list for the day, the week, or the month. Now ask yourself these questions:

How would I feel if my checklist didn't get accomplished today? Or tomorrow? Or next week?
How would I feel if I accomplished nothing?
How would I feel if today's plans collapsed?

My daily prayers have changed over the years. I used to ask God for protection for my family, help for the sick and lost, and would usually end with some thought like, "*Give me the strength to finish everything I need to do today.*"

Notice I said *need*. In actuality, most of my daily tasks were things I had taken on not out of need but out of a desire to be recognized or out of resentful obligation. Over time, God has gently revealed the motivations of my heart. Now, when I wake up, my morning prayer sounds like this: *"Lord, I love You. Thank You for Jesus. Thank You for blessing me far beyond what I deserve or could imagine. I don't care what happens today as long as You and I face it together."*

I'm slowly learning to let go of my need for acclaim. Inch by painful inch. I'm learning to crave His presence over my own performance.

THE PLAYGROUND

The older I get, the more it seems to me like our relationship with God resembles a child and parent at a playground. With God as my father, I'm running to the monkey bars, climbing them with unrestrained excitement. As I hang from the middle rung, my legs dangling, I shout, "Look, Daddy! Look what I can do!"

God grins and waves. "Good job, sweetie!"

Then I race to the slide, straining to reach the very top of the metal chute. At the pinnacle, I yell, "Look, Daddy! Look how high I am!"

God smiles again. "Wow! You're so big!"

Delighted with His praise, I then run to the swings, pumping my legs higher and higher until I can feel the wind in my face.

"Look at me, Daddy! I'm flying!"

God laughs. "You sure are. You're going to fly away like a bird any minute."

As God's kids, we race from activity to activity, filling our plates more and more to achieve the next thing, climb the next mountain, reach the next goal. We shout, "Look what I'm doing for You, Lord!" We're proud of our accomplishments, singing our own praises.

Yet for God, it's not about how fast we can climb, how high we can swing, or how amazing we are. We can't impress Him with our productivity or accomplishments. He spoke and mountains pushed up from flat sod. He breathed and wind swirled and formed, blowing gusts across the sea and land, scattering dandelions seeds across grass. He whispered and lightning slashed the sky with pewter light.

For Him, it's not about what we can do. It's about spending time together. It's about knowing each other. Laughing and learning and growing close. It's about shared memories and joy, tears, and lessons learned.

To put it another way, it's kind of like reading a biography of your favorite actor. For me, it's Jimmy Stewart. You memorize his birthdate, which college he attended, the names of his children, and his accomplishments. How many awards he won, how many movies he made. You even learn his favorite type of cookie and his favorite hobbies. Yet while your nose is buried in the book, you fail to realize Jimmy Stewart just walked into the room. You could be satisfied with learning about him, or you could put down the biography and talk to him one on one.

There is so much more to this life than a never-ending to-do list. So much more to enjoy than keeping our noses to the grindstone. Jesus Himself perfectly illustrated what His heart yearns to see in each of us.

> *As Jesus and the disciples continued on their way to Jerusalem, they came to a certain village where a woman named Martha welcomed him into her home. Her sister, Mary, sat at the Lord's feet, listening to what he taught. But Martha was distracted by the big dinner she was preparing. She came to Jesus and said, "Lord, doesn't it seem unfair to you that my sister just sits here while I do all the work? Tell her to come and help me." But the Lord said to her, "My dear Martha, you are worried and upset over all these details! There is only one thing worth being concerned about. Mary has discovered it, and it will not be taken away from her."*
> Luke 10:38–42, NLT

"Mary has discovered it." He's longing for us to discover it too.

BUMPER STICKERS

We've all seen the bumper stickers. "Proud parent of an honor roll student." There's nothing wrong with cheering our child along when they've done well, but how many of us are using our children's sports, academic achievements, or some other milestone to fill a hole inside ourselves? How many of us happily announce our kids' honor roll grades on social media, knowing deep down we will be praised for having such awesome offspring? If their exceptionalism reflects on us, then who couldn't help but praise us as well? And how many of us push our kids for the best grades possible because *we* can't face what it might mean to *us* if they fail?

Hard questions.

As someone whose son is on the autism spectrum, I've learned not to care when people stare because my son is clamping his ears and screaming because his overstimulated nervous system has reached its limit. I've learned that finding your worth through productivity is a myth. I've learned the greatest milestones to celebrate are the ones that often go unnoticed by others—when my son is readily accepted by a group of new children and when he manages to sit through a high school basketball game without crying. Those are personal victories for him. Victories that won't garner either of us worldwide fame but are huge markers on the path God has given us as we learn about Him and the gift of this life.

Personally, I'd like to see the bumper stickers changed up a bit. Maybe something like, "Proud parent of a child who showed love to the kid who's been bullying her" or "Rejoicing because my kid knows Jesus." Those are the standards that matter. Those are the ones that will change the world.

Our worth is in Jesus, not because of what we've done but because of what He's done. It's never been about us holding on to Him but His ability to hold on to us. When we embrace this truth, we can set aside the checklists and learn to be, instead of do.

BIBLE VERSE

"For I desire mercy, not sacrifice, and acknowledgment of God rather than burnt offerings." (Hosea 6:6, NIV)

READER TAKEAWAY

Working *for* God is not the same as being close *to* God. Productivity leads to exhaustion, but when we find our worth in our relationship with Jesus, we can rest.

THE TRUTH

God is more interested in having a relationship with us than having us do things for Him.

QUESTION

Consider a time you struggled with physical, emotional, or spiritual exhaustion. What do you believe caused it?

CHAPTER 3

The Lie of Perfectionism

The Disney princesses messed me up.

I confess I had quite a fascination with them when I was growing up—after I finished my Princess Leia phase, that is. I was going to be as beautiful as Aurora and have a grand adventure like Belle. And naturally I was going to be a singer like Ariel. Or, at the very least, a marine biologist.

But let's get real for a moment. There was one big problem with all those Disney beauties. They had no flaws.

Don't get me wrong. What made them such great heroines was their resilience in adversity, but they weren't real. They lived in a dreamy haze of melody-filled daydreams that somehow managed to blossom into perfect endings. No residual anger. No emotional baggage. No longstanding trauma.

Aurora (aka Sleeping Beauty) should have had abandonment issues, not to mention a prescription for narcolepsy. Cinderella was emotionally and physically abused yet never struggled with anger or fear. Belle married a guy with a bad temper and mood swings. Rapunzel was kidnapped and then married a convicted criminal. Snow White's stepmother tried to kill her.

Stephen Sondheim had some valuable insight in his hit Broadway musical *Into the Woods*. In this story, all the great fairytale characters' lives intersect: Jack from "Jack and the Beanstalk," Cinderella, Red Riding Hood, and Rapunzel. The first act is what you would imagine—beautiful arias full of hope and a longing to find their true love. And, of course, the act ends with them all finding their happily ever after.

But the second act of *Into the Woods* tells a different story. Cinderella and her prince are bored with each other. Red Riding Hood had such fun killing the wolf that she becomes a bloodthirsty hunter. Rapunzel suffers from depression from her past abuse. You get the idea.

I thought those Disney princesses with their perfect figures, perfect hair, perfect princes, and perfect endings meant I could be perfect too. But I'm not. Perfectionism is a lie that says, "To have worth, you must be flawless." It makes us work ourselves sick to attain the unattainable.

WHITEWASHED TOMBS

For many years, I lived the never-ending cycle of perfectionism. Everything looked perfect on the outside—perfect house, perfect marriage, perfect reputation—but eventually it all came crashing down. More on that to come.

It's impossible to be flawless 24/7. The cycle is exhausting, and even worse, it's fake. There is no authenticity. No vulnerability. No allowing myself to be me because I was focused on being someone I wasn't.

Weeks after that crash, as I sat in the rubble of who I once believed I was, I opened my Bible to Matthew 23. This is the passage where, as my grandmother often stated, Jesus let the Pharisees have it.

> *"Woe to you, teachers of the law and Pharisees, you hypocrites! You clean the outside of the cup and dish, but inside they are full of greed and self-indulgence. Blind Pharisee! First clean the inside of the cup and dish, and then the outside also will be clean. Woe to you, teachers of the law and Pharisees, you hypocrites! You are like whitewashed tombs, which look beautiful on the outside but on the inside are full of the bones of the dead and everything unclean. In the same way, on the outside you appear to people as righteous but on the inside you are full of hypocrisy and wickedness."* Matthew 23:25–28, NIV

Tremors wracked my body when I finished the passage, and that's when I realized I had been playacting my walk with God. On the outside, it looked like I had everything together, but inside I was an angry, resentful, hypocritical mess. I had tried to cover up my tumbled emotions by doing more for Jesus, but without examining my heart first, I just ended up exhausted, broken, and ashamed.

That day was a turning point in my walk with God. It began a long journey of being honest about who I am, opening my wounds to God's healing light, and learning to embrace the mess of imperfection.

Thankfully, I can say I am no longer a full-blown perfectionist but rather a recovering perfectionist. And if you are wondering, *recovering* simply means that at least I am aware of it now and am trying to heal.

Perfectionism can manifest itself in a variety of ways. I've expounded on a handful below.

A NEED FOR CONTROL

I've learned that much of my desire for perfection comes from a need for control. This doesn't mean that I run around bossing others with a scolding finger in their face. I see myself as a natural leader, and because circumstances beyond my control affected me deeply when I was younger, I tend to turn to control to maintain a sense of security and normalcy.

Control provides us with the illusion of a sense of certainty, of being able to predict what will happen in the future, of consistency when it comes to the people in our lives, and of achieving perfect peace in a messy world. Let me stop here and say that control provides the *illusion* of certainty and security, but that is often not reality. For example, I don't like spontaneity. It makes my stomach cramp. If I could schedule a time to be spontaneous, then I would. Having a change in my plans threatens my feelings of security and well-being. Life suddenly becomes scary and unsafe when I have too many surprises in a day. So I spend an inordinate amount of time worrying over all the things that *could* happen, and then I try to head them off before they occur.

THE NEED FOR APPROVAL

If you are a perfectionist, you may have learned early in life that other people valued you because of how much you accomplished or achieved. As a result, you may have learned to value yourself only based on other people's approval. This can leave you vulnerable and overly sensitive to the opinions and criticism of others. The only way I can protect myself from criticism is to never fail. And that is a very heavy load to carry.

FEAR OF FAILURE AND MAKING MISTAKES

For some reason, in my mind, mistakes often equal failure, but that is not true. Mistakes provide us with opportunities to learn, to grow, to be creative. And failing to achieve a goal does not mean I don't have value. It just means I'm human.

Many perfectionists think in terms of black and white. It's a way of living at the extremes—either all or nothing—with no room for the gray. A straight "A" student who receives a "B" might believe they are a failure.

In addition, perfectionists often feel consumed with *shoulds*. I *should* read my Bible. I *should* go to church. I *should* love that person who is driving me crazy. The problem with *shoulds* is that they stress obedience without proper motivation.

FEAR OF DISAPPROVAL

For many perfectionists, being broken equals loss of love, so they try their hardest to hide their flaws and work their hardest to keep everyone around them happy. Often, perfectionism and people-pleasing go hand in hand.

Perfectionists live in a vicious cycle. First, they set lofty goals that are incredibly hard to reach. The constant pressure to perform leads to anxiety and reduces their ability to work effectively. Then they fail to reach those goals because they were unrealistic to begin with. That's when the self-criticism and guilt begin to chip away at their mental and emotional state until they are knee deep in inner turmoil. Yet they think, *Maybe if I try harder, I'll succeed*, which sets the whole washing machine spinning again.

COMPARISON

I've often heard the adage "Comparison is the thief of joy." How true. An antelope doesn't compete with a caterpillar on achievement or status, nor does an iris glance longingly at a tulip and think, *I wish I were more like her.* Creation simply *is.* Cells multiply, stars twinkle, flowers bloom, and rain falls because that's what they were created to do.

We humans, however, are different. The problem with comparison is we don't compare two things with unbiased judgment. It's an unbalanced scale. We judge our own value and compare it against others' social media highlight reels. We either look down our noses and say, "Well, at least I don't mess up like *her*," or we compare our achievements to the shining, gleaming trophies of others. "I'll never be as good as she is." Neither statement is true.

Without even realizing it, perfectionists may unintentionally apply their high standards to family and friends in their circle, becoming critical, demanding, or resentful. They usually try to keep others from seeing their mistakes, not realizing that honesty and the ability to be real are qualities that are attractive to others. They hide who they truly are and oftentimes suffer from strained and distant personal relationships. Worse yet, they apply those same unattainable standards to their children.

We've all seen the mom screaming at the child who failed to hit that home run in the last inning of the big game or the dad fuming at his kid who came in second after leading for the first three laps around the track. The shame they heap upon their little one is shocking—not because the child failed but because they feel the child made *them* look bad. Their reaction teaches their offspring one lasting, crushing lesson. That love—or at least their parents' love—is conditional.

Perfectionism is buying into the lie that we are not enough. That our kids are not enough. That somehow, by achieving more, gaining recognition and acclaim, we can somehow soothe that aching loss inside. It may work for a little while—until the one time you or your loved one doesn't measure up.

Getting down to the heart of the matter is this: we all crave unconditional love.

Those Disney princesses craved unconditional love too, with their ideal of the perfect prince who would give them a perfect future and a perfect, unselfish love. But the only One who can give us all those things is Jesus Christ. Yet we all continue to look for unconditional love in conditional people.

WHEN THE MAKEUP RUNS

Getting back to those pesky princesses, I recently came face to face with one. Kind of.

Not long ago, our family visited Disney World in Florida. I watched the performers dancing down Main Street of Magic Kingdom, spinning in their glittering, satin costumes, smiling with those perfectly straight white teeth and painted lips, and I couldn't help it. I felt a pang of pity.

They were beautiful and mesmerizing as they sang and danced under the swelling rush of orchestra music and confetti. Every little girl wanted to be like those singing princesses. Every boy wanted to be as courageous as those muscled, grinning princes. Their exuberant performances drew everyone's attention as the crush of people applauded and whistled their approval. Oh, but I forgot to mention that this day was hot. Very hot.

To a casual observer, these performers were having a ball—unless you got a glimpse of them up close. I did.

One particular princess danced by, grinning and waving. I was on the edge of the street with a particularly good view as she pranced toward the children at my side. That's when I saw it: her make-up was running in streams down her face. Her mascara was melting, leaving shadowy puddles under her eyes. Even her wig was askew from the sweat soaking her head. Why, she wasn't a blonde at all! She was a brunette. Neither was her skin flawlessly smooth but red and splotchy from the heat. Her eyes met mine, and I saw a flicker of something akin to exhaustion. Weariness. But as soon as the glimmer appeared, it was snuffed out, safely tucked back into hiding beneath the mask of a perfectly carefree princess.

I instantly felt a tug of sympathy. Memories of my time in college working for my performance degree assaulted me; the fatigue, the demands. Performance after performance, hour after hour, day after day. No room for mistakes despite weather, illness, or personal circumstances. That's how I've lived my life ever since.

As I caught that tiny glimpse of a crack in her mask, what truly hurt my heart was the knowledge that *I've been there on a deeper level as well, and it's far more devastating than dancing in the scorching Florida sun. It's the charade of trying to be a perfect person.*

Always smile. Hide the pain. Do what anyone asks of you. Win their approval. If they are happy with you, they'll never see what a mess you are inside. They'll never know about that addiction or secret shame. Do more. Be more. You can't mess up. If you do, you'll lose their respect, approval, and, worst of all, their love.

So instead of letting folks see us and know us in all our messiness, we cover our flaws and our need to be loved with a cloak of Christianity. Just serve. Smile. Pretend. Sing and dance.

Yet too many of us are miserable inside, desperate to shed our costumes and pretense.

It's all about making people think we are something other than we truly are. At best, it's play acting. A charade. At worst, it's nothing less than living a lie. Hypocrisy. Deception.

Ouch.

How many of us are playacting our walk with God, trying to pretend like we have it together but are a trembling, resentful bundle of brokenness inside? How many of us think that if people saw our true selves they could never love us? How many of us are exhausted from trying to be perfect but never reaching the mark?

Sometimes our busyness and perfectly executed activities, our lying smiles, and the furor of pretending generates a heat so hot, our masterful application of thick makeup runs in rivulets of sweat, stripping away the rosy cheeks to reveal the pale flesh beneath. The mask melts and runs.

Stated another way, there are only two options with perfectionism—keep striving to attain what isn't possible, spinning like an exhausted hamster on the proverbial wheel, or crack from the strain of being something you're not.

I get it. I really do. I've always known God loves me unconditionally, but people? That's a whole other issue. People are fickle, mean, wishy-washy, demanding, and unfair. Which begs the question: why are so many of us killing ourselves to be perfect in order to win the conditional approval of people who are just as messy as we are?

I think many of us confuse approval with love. Approval is a stamp given by someone else that says, "You meet my expectations." Love says, "You're a broken mess, and I love you anyway." They are polar opposites.

When we finally stop trying to be something we're not and focus on what Christ has done for us, He comes and gently wipes away all that makeup we've tried so desperately to hide behind. Those crushing, suffocating demands fall away, and we finally taste freedom for the first time. No more masks. No more pretending.

The acceptance of One who loves you exactly as you are is like being cut free from dragging around two hundred pounds of iron chains. The burden is light. Trying to be perfect to win human approval snaps those chains right back onto your body. Anytime we replace God with a poor substitute, we suffer. Period.

Don't be afraid to wipe off your makeup. There's a pretty awesome person underneath. Jesus must have thought so as well. After all, He came to redeem you and has a distinct plan for your life—a plan that doesn't include you trying to be something or someone you're not.

He loves you, imperfections and all.

BROKEN THINGS

"Shouldn't you get a new phone?"

I've heard the question countless times. I suppose it's a reasonable remark considering the state of my cracked phone screen. How the multiple shards of glass have managed to keep from falling out or cutting my fingers is a mystery. Still, since that wild day when God grabbed hold of my heart, the question rankles me. Why? The phone works just fine despite its cracked appearance.

We are obsessed with perfection. If something is broken, we just toss it away and replace it with a new model. A better one.

Sometimes our attitude about objects bleeds into the way we treat people too. What a tragedy.

I battled epilepsy as a child. I'll never forget the shame that accompanied those moments in elementary school when I would find two dozen pairs of eyes staring at me in horror because I had had a seizure. I remember how frustrating it was to find a chunk of time yawning like a black hole in my memory. And I remember the helplessness of having no control over my own body.

Fast forward to the present, and life hasn't changed. We all deal with tough stuff: poor health, children with special needs, the slicing pain of divorce, rejection, depleted bank accounts, or angry coworkers. For some, the most devastating blow of all is being forgotten by your children. For others, you might be dealing with the mess from your own poor decisions, and you just need a little grace from people unwilling to give it. Whatever the situation, we're far from perfect. Messy. Broken. We wonder, *How can God possibly use me now?*

Our culture has glamorized what the world defines as "perfect." From the airbrushed models gracing the latest covers of *Vogue,* to the highlight reels inundating social media, we are constantly told we must be flawless to be accepted. The flip side of that lie is that anything broken must be rejected.

If we build our identity on something other than Christ—whether it's our appearance, social reputation, prestige, beauty, or a picture-perfect home, — the greater the pain when that identity crumbles.

Perfection and value are not the same thing. Neither are brokenness and worth. As James Hewett writes, "God uses broken things. It takes broken soil to produce a crop, broken clouds to give rain, broken grain to give bread, broken bread to give strength. It is the broken alabaster box that gives forth perfume . . . it is Peter, weeping bitterly, who returns to greater power than ever."[5]

A pivotal moment in my life occurred when I overheard a conversation between two former friends. One of them was whispering about me at a party, unaware I was standing quietly in the corner nearby.

"Tara acts like she has it all together, but I know she doesn't. She couldn't. Someday, all of her pretending is going to be exposed. And honestly, pretending to be perfect is annoying."

The second friend agreed, and they laughed together, unaware I heard every barbed word.

Ouch.

The truth hurt, more deeply than I thought possible, but I needed that wake-up call.

Perfection isn't attractive. Vulnerability is. Pretending is never as valuable as honesty. My worth isn't found in being flawless, but in knowing Jesus is crazy about me, cracks and all. Even better, He prefers to work through my imperfections.

> *Each time he said, "My grace is all you need. My power works best in weakness." So now I am glad to boast about my weaknesses, so that the power of Christ can work through me.*
> 2 Corinthians 12:9, NLT

All my life, I've heard it said that broken things are special because the cracks allow the light to come in. I don't believe that's true. As a child of God, brokenness allows the Light to shine out.

When we put on a mask of perfection, we're only allowing people to see a plastic version of who we really are. Brokenness allows the mask to be stripped away. Pretense is gone. All that is left is honesty, humility and fractures of space where self has been emptied so others can see Jesus shining through. Best-selling author Bob Goff says it best in his book *Love Does*: "It has always seemed to me that broken things, just like broken people, get used more; it's probably because God has more pieces to work with."[6]

Despite my struggle, I have learned one very important thing: perfect is boring. For me, flawless has become synonymous with plastic. Dull. Lifeless. What a miserable way to live. No, I think I'll strive for the biblical definition of perfect instead: *complete*. Complete in Jesus. Whole. Not lacking anything because His grace has filled the broken places where my own weakness is laid bare.

BREAKING PERFECTIONISM

Now that we recognize the problem, and see what causes it, what will we do about it?

It's important to remember that God loves us no matter how well—or how poorly—we perform.

> *In all these things we are more than conquerors through him who loved us. For I am convinced that neither death nor life, neither angels nor demons, neither the present nor the future, nor any powers, neither height nor depth, nor anything else in all creation, will be able to separate us from the love of God that is in Christ Jesus our Lord.* Romans 8:37–39, NIV

We did nothing to earn His love, and there is nothing we can do to lose it. At the end of our lives, we will not stand before our peers; we'll stand before Him. Pleasing Him is all that matters, and He has already declared us loved and worthy.

In remembering how much we're loved and how much He values us, we have to remind ourselves that we will mess up. We're human. We are imperfect creatures who will let others down at some point. When it happens, the best course of action is to confess it to the Lord, ask forgiveness from the one we've wronged, and move on.

KINTSUGI

Over the past few years, I have studied the philosophy of *kintsugi*. This is a Japanese art form that embraces the beauty of flaws and imperfections.

For most of society, when something breaks, like the screen of my cell phone, we toss it away because broken means worthless, right?

Not so.

Japanese artisans look at broken things in a different way. When a bowl or a cup or plate breaks, they gather all the broken pieces and gently bind the fragments back together using liquid gold. The result is an object with veins of beauty running throughout its form. It's no longer the original but infinitely more interesting and with more character than it ever had before being broken.

That's what Jesus does. He takes our mess and binds it back into wholeness with His love and light. The marks reveal a journey, a story that cannot be untold, but is infinitely more captivating than that original "perfect" version.

There is no story with perfection, no enthralling tale from plastic things. But something broken? That's where the beauty lies.

BROKEN IS BEAUTIFUL

As I have learned to let go of perfection and be truthful about who I am and how I struggle, a whole new world of authenticity has opened up to me. I have deep friendships forged in honesty. We're not flawless, but we're real. The people I once longed to impress with my perfect life have slowly disappeared, but the friends in my current circle are delightfully truthful. We don't pretend. We share our true selves and in so doing, we have infused each other with hope and courage. Instead of being alone in my illusion of perfection, I'm connected to people who know their worth in Christ. As Brené Brown states in her book *Rising Strong*, "Vulnerability is not winning or losing; it's having the courage to show up and be seen when we have no control over the outcome. Vulnerability is not weakness; it's our greatest measure of courage."[7]

My own pitiful efforts to live an impeccable life failed, as they do for every human, but my hope no longer rests in my attempts to be perfect. My future and my worth are held in the nail-scarred hands of Jesus. I don't have to be perfect because He has already completed it for me.

Life isn't a fairy tale, as I once believed, but I've discovered true beauty—and it is unearthed in the broken places.

BIBLE VERSE

"Woe to you, teachers of the law and Pharisees, you hypocrites! You clean the outside of the cup and dish, but inside they are full of greed and self-indulgence. Blind Pharisee! First clean the inside of the cup and dish, and then the outside also will be clean." (Matthew 23:25–26, NIV)

READER TAKEAWAY

Hiding behind a mask of perfectionism always fails at some point. Just as we see in the art of *kintsugi*, there is great beauty in imperfection and brokenness.

THE TRUTH

We cannot hide our broken places from God. He sees us yet loves us immeasurably.

QUESTION

How does our culture try to convince us that perfection is attainable?

CHAPTER 4
The Lie of People-Pleasing

One Christmas, I was asked to sing a solo for the church choir cantata. I had been struggling with allergy problems, and the song in question boasted a high note that landed in the upper atmosphere. Knowing it would be hard to pull off with my current voice problems, I asked the director if I could rework the melody in that phrase and opt for a lower note. He happily agreed.

At the next rehearsal, a choir member approached me, complaining about the change we'd made. "That song is so beautiful with that big high note in the middle of it! You've got to do it the way it's written." Now, I'm ornery enough that when someone tells me I *have to* do something, I immediately want to do the opposite. Oblivious to my irritation, he continued, "Don't you trust God to help you hit that note?"

Ouch. My determination to do what was best for me faltered. Was I not trusting God to help me? Maybe I wasn't looking at this from the right spiritual angle. Was I doubting God?

Then this man landed the final blow in my spirit. He said, "If you love God, you can claim Philippians 4:13 (NKJV): 'I can do all things through Christ who strengthens me.'" He smiled and patted me on the shoulder before walking away. I stood rooted to the spot, wrestling indecision.

The evening of the cantata I was filled with anxiety and doubt. I decided this man made a valid point, and more than anything else, I didn't want to let anyone down. So I reached for the high note—and my voice cracked. I wanted to crawl under the pew in embarrassment. I sat down with a red face and begged Jesus to come back immediately.

Can you see what this guy did to manipulate me? First, he tried to fix things the way *he* thought they should be. He refused to understand my reasons. He questioned my faith in God and then used scripture to manipulate me into doing something I knew I couldn't do. This kind of tactic is called *spiritual manipulation*. That's one of the problems people pleasers face: we become magnets for boundary abusers.

Although the manipulator in this story must bear the responsibility for what he said, I wish I had stood up for myself. Instead, I tried to keep him happy. In this case, I could have said no, but I chose not to.

A SNEAKY LIE

People-pleasing is tricky to detect. It looks like love and kindness. It appears to others like the giving friend, the ideal wife, or the dedicated employee. The people pleaser gives their all to any project placed before them and often volunteers to take on the tasks no one else will touch. They excel at whatever they do. They are sensitive to the needs of others, go the extra mile, and are often extremely organized. They meet each challenge with a can-do attitude. Sounds good, right? But to understand the lie of people-pleasing, we have to dig below the surface.

Because people pleasers are so sensitive to the needs of others, they often neglect themselves and their own families. They appear kind but are often filled with resentment and anger. They take on responsibility while battling exhaustion each day. They want to seem like they have it all together. They have trouble saying "no," so they say "yes" while wondering how on earth they'll be able to fulfill the obligation. They need constant approval and are often chained to people's expectations (or perceived expectations).

The lie of people-pleasing tells us that approval and love are the same thing. To be loved, we must please others—even at our own expense.

TOMATOES

I desperately want people to like me.

There. I said it. The thought of someone being displeased with me in any way feels like a cold stone being dropped in my gut. And conflict? Count me out.

What's one way to shake that miserable feeling of dread? Work harder. Be more agreeable, more likable. Fit in, because if they find out what you're really like, their acceptance will disappear. Right?

That's what I told myself, anyways.

I've battled people-pleasing all my life. I can readily admit that now, but I would have died a thousand deaths to confess such a thing ten years ago. At one point, my people-pleasing was so intrusive that I couldn't even express my own tastes for fear of someone thinking I was odd. One day, my friends were chatting about how much they loved fresh tomatoes.

One of them turned to me with smile, asking, "Is there anything more delicious than a fresh tomato, Tara?"

I replied, "Of course not! Nothing better."

Confession: I hate tomatoes with a passion.

Why did I lie? Especially over something so trivial? Because I craved acceptance. I needed their love. And I mistakenly thought that disagreement led to loss of love.

At the time I told the "tomato lie," I did anything that anyone asked me to do. I exhausted myself to make others happy, and it left me perpetually angry on the inside.

GLORIOUS MARTYRDOM

Have you ever been around someone who sees themselves as a martyr? Or maybe you've fallen into the trap of martyrdom at some point. I know I have. I've found myself wallowing in my suffering, believing I have no control over my situation. I've felt like a poor, afflicted soul who is put upon by others. I've felt misunderstood and have suffered in silence. But this mentality left me stuck with the perfect excuse not to look at my own behavior. It let me believe that I have no responsibility in my own decisions or future.

The truth? Martyrdom is a choice.

But what does martyrdom have to do with people-pleasing? The two are intimately linked. While martyrdom sounds noble, heroic even, it actually means we are the victim of other people's bad decisions. People pleasers often view their role in the same way. "People just don't understand how I tired I am." "Why does he always call on me to bail him out at the last minute?" "Why am I always the one giving?" People pleasers feel bound to being "nice" and agreeable, often at their own physical, emotional, and spiritual expense. Though people pleasers think they are giving themselves away for the good of others, the truth is that their prime motivation is fear. And, ultimately, people pleasers begin to experience resentment and anger over time. Like a forest fire, it starts subtly but soon grows into an inferno.

So why would anyone choose it?

THE CHECKLIST

If you're still not sure if you're a closet people pleaser, here is an easy way to gauge the possibility. This checklist isn't exhaustive by any stretch, but it's a good starting place. Consider how many of the following questions you would answer "Yes" to:

Do you find it nearly impossible to say "no" to a request?

Do you ever feel responsible for the mood of others?

Do you tell people what they want to hear to avoid conflict?

Do you feel like it is your responsibility to keep others happy?

Do you often find yourself responsible for tasks that you really don't want to do?

Do you feel uneasy about the decisions you've made until you receive approval from others?

Do you find yourself bending over backward to get people to like you? Even if you don't really like them?

Do you struggle to say no to someone without feeling the need to explain yourself?

Have you ever had an opinion different from your group of peers but kept your opinion quiet because you feared rejection?

Do you apologize excessively?

Do you ever feel resentment toward people who make requests of your time and/or talent?

After being at a party or other social event, do you replay conversations you had with others over and over in your mind?

Do you constantly worry that something you said might have offended someone?

This list makes me squirm like a worm in hot ashes, mainly because at one time in life, I could answer a resounding "Yes" to all of these questions. For me, the hard part was figuring out why.

THE LIE

If you ask psychologists what causes people-pleasing to develop, you'll hear things like trauma, anxiety, abuse, unmet emotional needs, and more, but none of those explanations fit for my own situation. I had to do much reflection and soul-searching to find the answer.

I was raised as a preacher's kid, and something I noticed about people from a young age is that we humans tend to pick each other apart. We attack those who think differently than we do, those who buck the norms, and those who convict us of our own issues.

Since I despise conflict, my solution was to spot a potential problem and do everything I could to diffuse the tension with a smile, a joke, or a solution. Somehow, I got it in my mind that God was happy when people were happy, and, according to my skewed observations, people were happy when I put on a "good girl" persona and did whatever anyone asked of me. Part of this warped thinking occurred because I was so highly praised when I bent over backward to make people relax. "Tara, you're such a good helper." "Your good attitude makes everyone so happy." "We don't know what we would do without you." On and on it went. For a person who thrives on verbal praise, the attention was like a drug.

To make matters worse, my concentration on being "the obedient kid" morphed into an obsession with obeying *everyone*.

Most of us have been told to be obedient since we were babies. "I need you to obey Mommy." "Don't give me that look." "Clean your room and I'll give you ice cream." Combine that with all the verses, Bible stories, and sermons about obeying, and it's easy to see why some of us become hypervigilant about it. Abraham obeyed God. Joseph obeyed. Jesus obeyed. Jesus even said, "If you love me, obey my commandments" (John 14:15, NLT). Obedience is crucial and critical to walking with God. However, the problem comes when we switch God's commands for people's commands. Just because someone asks for your help or insists they know what you should be doing does not mean they are declaring God's plans for your life. Human demands do not equal the will of God.

As I grew, these people-pleasing tendencies exploded and became a way of life. I needed the attention and accolades. I craved it. And somewhere along the way, I embraced the lie that approval equals love. It took me years to realize they are not the same thing.

Approval is a stamp someone gives you that says, "You meet my expectations." Love says, "You are a hot mess, and I'm crazy about you anyway." Approval is based on performance. Love is based on identity. Approval is lost when we fail or say "no." Love is unconditional—there is nothing you can do to earn it and nothing you can do to lose it. Approval and love are polar opposites.

APPROVAL ADDICTION

Some psychologists say that people-pleasing is an addiction. It sure felt that way to me when I was at my worst. Seeing someone's smile, knowing I had somehow gained their approval was like a high, a feeling I needed to repeat over and over. Why?

Addicts often feel like they have no control. Same with people pleasers. We do everything we can to minimize that anxious feeling.

Addicts have a need/hate relationship with their issue. They need it to feel good about themselves, but they despise the fact that they need it at all. Same with people pleasers, especially when you consider the silent resentment we aim at those who continually make demands of our time.

Addicts know the high from their substance is fleeting. Same for people pleasers. Approval feels amazing when it's given but leaves exhaustion in its wake.

Addicts battle feelings of hopelessness. It's the same for people pleasers. We don't know how to crawl out of the hole we've created. The more we do, the more is expected of us, and the more exhausted we feel. It's a vicious cycle.

For these reasons, I often describe people pleasers as "approval addicts."

IMPRESSIONS

My kids love impressions. The crazier, the better. And being a singer, I always find it a hilarious exercise to see if I can manipulate my voice enough to oblige their whims.

One day I spent all day conversing like the Queen of Hearts from *Alice in Wonderland*. When bad manners were displayed at dinner, the Queen of Hearts yelled, "Off with your head!" which caused an eruption of giggles.

I have spent much time as the Count from *Sesame Street*, Patrick from *Spongebob Squarepants*, Maria from *The Sound of Music*, Elmyra from *Tiny Toons*, Ethel Merman, Glinda from *Wicked*, not to mention a cast of unique quirky characters created by our crazy family. It makes me wonder what impression my kids will pick the next day and if I'll be able to pull it off.

One time they begged me to talk like the singer Adele. And when I say that they asked me to converse like Adele, I mean all day long. Around the clock for two weeks. I used my Cockney accent so frequently that I forgot what my own voice sounded like.

The funny thing is that after I spent a few days talking like Adele, I couldn't stop. Pretending became the norm. The norm became habit. And habit became hard to break. I forgot my own voice. And pretending to be someone I wasn't made me feel like I was constantly in performance mode.

To put it another way, psychotherapist Santiago Delboy said this about a client who struggled with people-pleasing and self-inflicted martyrdom: "The people-pleasing chameleon ends up becoming invisible. By shifting colors to match its environment, the chameleon disappears. By engaging in people-pleasing to match someone else's needs, [his client] disappeared as well. This led her to an impossible situation: To get the validation she sought, she needed to not be herself."[8]

Too many of us live in an illusion meant to fool others and hide our true selves. We don't like people seeing us in all of our messiness and brokenness. So we stay tucked behind our impressions. We give people what we think they want to hear and lose who God wants us to be in the process. We become chameleons, changing our color to blend in and survive.

And that's what people-pleasing is: a desperate attempt to avoid rejection and pain.

The praise we generate from people-pleasing might be fun for a little while, but we can't live there. God has a unique plan for our lives, and we can't be authentic if we're living a lie, trying to be someone we're not. God loves us, not the masks we wear or the performances we display to be accepted, no matter how stellar our Adele impressions may be.

THE HEART OF THE MATTER

When I eventually hit rock bottom, which most approval addicts do, a friend pointed out that I had been living my life as if people meant more to me than God. In my daily Bible study, I ran across a verse that I had read many times before, but it pierced my heart in a completely different way: "Am I now trying to win the approval of human beings, or of God? Or am I trying to please people? If I were still trying to please people, I would not be a servant of Christ." (Galatians 1:10, NIV)

That caught my attention. Who was I really living for—people or God? The answer is neither. When you strip down all the fluff and distraction of agreeableness, who I was really living for was myself.

The root of people-pleasing is not love. It's fear. Fear of rejection. Fear of abandonment. In reality, people-pleasing is based in pride because we break our backs to do for others, but we're really doing it is to make ourselves feel better. It looks like fruit of the spirit, but it's actually self-serving. This lie breeds idol worship of others. Some would even argue it's worship of self because it's self-preservation. It enables us to put someone or something else before God. In the middle of uncovering my own struggle, I realized my actions were telling Jesus that what everyone else thought about me was more important than what He thought.

Jesus is not a people pleaser. He's a God pleaser. When He walked this earth, He did the will of His Father and nothing more. If I want to mold my life to look like His, I need to do the same.

To take it one step further, Jesus is the One who died to save us. When this life is over, we won't stand before a jury of our peers. We'll stand before Him. Pleasing Him is all that matters.

Here is the good news: we can break the cycle. Our condition does not have to be our conclusion. So how do we break free?

PRETENDERS

I opened the mailbox and rifled through the collection of papers waiting to be opened.

Bills, bills, junk mail, bills…I stopped when one brightly colored advertisement caught my eye. Clutched in my fingers was the smiling face of Dolly Parton.

I scanned the ad, admiring the bright, glossy sheen. Dolly Parton was coming to my hometown? Why hadn't I heard about this? Miss Islands-in-the-Stream-I-Will-Always-Love-You was coming to my city next week? Why wasn't this being blasted from every television and radio station in town? Someone of her acclaim should be welcomed with more than a flyer. No fanfare or hoopla?

I studied the flyer again, and that's when I caught it. The name Dolly Parton was in big, bold letters. Underneath in teeny, timid font was the word *Impersonator*.

It went on to list the impersonator's name and accolades, but I was no longer interested. With a shrug, I tossed the flyer in the trash, wondering how the venue could possibly fill the number of seats available in only a week.

Why did I toss the flyer? Because no matter how wonderful the impersonator was, no matter how talented or how close she looked or sang to the legend, she was not the real Dolly Parton. I was interested in the actual artist, not a pretender.

Fake is never as valuable as the real thing.

Living for approval, for that stamp of acceptance from your peers will turn you into a fake. Oh, you might be a great one. You might be able to sound and look like the real thing. But just because something looks like the real thing doesn't mean it is.

How many of us give up our status as a diamond in the King's crown only to spend our resources pretending to be cubic zirconium instead? Anyone who knows the difference between the two can easily tell you the diamond is infinitely more precious. Why do we spend our lives trying to be something we're not? The simple answer is that we don't see our own worth.

> *For we are His workmanship [His own master work, a work of art], created in Christ Jesus [reborn from above—spiritually transformed, renewed, ready to be used] for good works, which God prepared [for us] beforehand [taking paths which He set], so that we would walk in them [living the good life which He prearranged and made ready for us].*
> Ephesians 2:10, AMP

When we live for approval, when we become plastic people, we are throwing away the beautiful purpose designed for us before we were ever born. What a tragedy.

The world already has a Dolly Parton—and there is only one you. Only one person with your unique fingerprint. Only one person with your unique blend of talents, skills, and quirks. Don't throw away your worth pretending to be something different.

BREAKING FREE

The first step toward breaking free of people-pleasing is to confess your feelings to God. He already knows how exhausted you are, how you struggle with needing acceptance. He sees it all, but there is tremendous peace in laying your soul bare before Him so healing can begin.

The second step takes a bit longer. Try to unearth the source of your approval addiction. This takes courage. Ask yourself about your motives. Why do you do what you do?

And then after you have figured that out, dig deeper. I'll show you what I mean.

Not long ago, I read *Inside Out* by Larry Crabb, which God used to teach me a lot about my own motives. Although I'm very friendly and have a few close friends, I tend to hold most people at a distance. When the phone rings, I want to run, even without knowing who is on the other end. So I asked myself why. Here is how that internal conversation went:

> *I want to run because it might be someone who will want me to do something for them.*
>
> *Would that be so bad?*
>
> *Not necessarily. But I've had bad experiences with needy people. In the past, they have taken advantage of me. They don't respect my boundaries and that sucks my energy dry.*
>
> *Why do you think that is?*
>
> *I just told you why! I'm a people pleaser!*
>
> *Dig deeper. What if it isn't someone wanting you to give you a to-do list? What if it is just someone wanting to chat?*
>
> *I still want to run away from that ringing phone.*
>
> *Why? Dig deeper.*

Close friendships scare me.

Why?

Because if they get close to me, they might see how broken I really am inside. They will think less of me. They won't love me anymore.

See what I mean?

I believe that if we are fearless enough to be honest, to search our hearts and ask God to shine His light on our brokenness, He will reveal groundbreaking and life-changing awareness to our minds and spirits. And He can transform us to be people who live in freedom, no longer chained to the cycle of people-pleasing and its lies.

DITCHING THE DOORMAT

The common ground sought by people pleasers the world over is a desperate need to feel loved. We search for unconditional love in conditionally minded people. We crave approval, using it as a gauge to tell us our own worth.

Somewhere along the way, I took my eyes off Jesus and began living for the applause of people. Men and women just like me. Sinners and failures, just like me. People who have made a mess of their own lives, just like me. People who didn't die for me, yet I esteemed their opinion as if they did. And I lost sight of my Savior in the process. I gave away freedom and unconditional love and traded them for hopelessness and conditions.

I'm tired of shackling myself to others' expectations when obeying Him is all that matters. I'm tired of being sucked into a spiral of exhaustion when He has promised me rest. I'm tired of living like everyone else's opinion of me is more important than

His. I have no desire to make people, and their approval, my idol, my focus, or my hope any longer.

But all that matters is what God thinks—and He loved us so much, He gave His own life to redeem us from the land of darkness. It doesn't matter whether we're on top of the world or scraping bottom at our worst; His love never changes.

And I've discovered this amazing truth is what my heart has been searching for all along.

BIBLE VERSE

Am I now trying to win the approval of human beings, or of God? Or am I trying to please people? If I were still trying to please people, I would not be a servant of Christ. (Galatians 1:10, NIV)

READER TAKEAWAY

Living a life of people-pleasing in the name of doing things for God cannot be sustained. Eventually our masks will crumble, but God is gracious to reveal our true motives with gentleness and love.

THE TRUTH

Approval and love are not the same thing. God loves us unconditionally, so there is no need to seek approval from people.

QUESTION

What are your motives for serving others? Do you give out of love or for other reasons, like obligation, being seen, accolades, or because you fear what will happen if you say "no"? How difficult is it for you to say "no"?

CHAPTER 5

The Lie of Depression

I stared at the drumsticks in my hand, struggling to focus on my professor's instructions.

"OK, guys. We're doing 'Unforgettable.' David, you'll take the guitar solo. No saxophone on this one. Tara, try sticks first, but we may switch to brushes the next time through."

I nodded. Brushes. No, sticks. Which one was I supposed to use first again?

"Brian, remember to keep the bass consistent. It will be a difficult balance for you because we're taking it in a slow swing. You need to lead without driving the song."

My jazz professor's words slowly faded as I stared at the gray walls of our rehearsal room. The brick walls were gray. The chairs were gray. I peered out the window into the gloomy January sky. Gray.

I sighed and returned to stare at the battered white head of the snare drum brushing my knees. Blank. Empty.

I tried to shake away the fog. I just needed sleep. That was all. I mentally calculated how long I'd slept the night before.

Eight hours? Ten? My days were blurring, resembling a watercolor with no distinct lines. I used to be able to easily run on six hours of sleep. Why couldn't I get enough now?

"Alright." My professor's voice snapped my focus back to the present. He lifted his hands. "And one, and two, and three, and four."

The instruments launched into a soothing, moody rendition of the Nat King Cole classic, but I couldn't seem to find my groove. Was I following the bass player, or was he following me? I closed my eyes, the drumsticks unyielding in my fingers. I was holding them too tight.

Relax, Tara.

But I couldn't. I lost track of the meter. One, two, three—no. I was on four, and the others were on two. I blew out a breath and tried to listen to the guitars. I searched for the lyrics. "Like a song of love that clings to me . . ."

Concentrate on the words, and your brain will match them to the chords. Find your groove.

But in the blink of an eye, the lyrics fled my mind too. What song were we doing again?

You just need sleep. That's all.

"Unforgettable." I nearly laughed at the absurdity of it. I had forgotten we were rehearsing the song "Unforgettable." Ridiculous. Why couldn't I think?

Somehow, I fumbled my way through the rest of the rehearsal, but tears burned the backs of my eyes. When our professor declared our practice session over, I heaved a thick sigh and moved to put the drumsticks where they belonged. A warm hand squeezed my shoulder. I looked into my professor's face. His blue eyes were flooded with concern.

"Tara, are you OK?"

Was I? I was a singer and pianist. I could compose music and even improvised on drums, but today...today I couldn't. In truth, I didn't even care. All I wanted was to sleep and relax into oblivion. And that scared me more than anything else.

Tears blurred his image as I shook my head. "No, I'm not. There's something wrong with me."

It was 2002. And if I were honest, I would have admitted life had been wrong for a very long time.

2002

Most people have a year they look back on and say, "Now that was *the* year." It could be a year of joy, of intense pain, of heartache, or of kicking down hard-fought obstacles. For me, 2002 was the year that drove me to my knees. I had believed so many lies, exhausted myself into the ground, and was nothing but a wad of conflicting emotions.

Looking back, I can see the signs so easily: lack of concentration, lack of motivation. No matter how deeply I set my mind to do something, my ability to focus fluttered around like a moth near a security light. But I wasn't hyper either. Each morning, I forced myself out of bed. It wasn't that I was melancholy or just wanted some extra down time. It took every amount of grit and determination I had just to rise in the morning.

At first, I noticed a little fatigue. Then I found myself feeling exhausted day after day. Before too long, seven or eight hours of sleep wouldn't do. Then it was nine hours, ten hours—but the more I slept, the more exhausted I became.

I attended college classes, ate meals, worked in the music department at my school, attended church services, but all I could think was *When can I go to sleep?* Every night I collapsed into bed, hoping the cool sheets would relieve my exhaustion. Nothing sounded like fun. I couldn't laugh and joke. Activities I had enjoyed previously like reading, writing, singing, playing piano, or painting held absolutely no interest. My life held no color or vibrancy. Everything was bland shades of gray.

But most of all I wanted to escape, leave all responsibilities behind and run. And I didn't know how.

THE BATHMAT

I'll never forget the night in 2002 when I told God, "I want out."

I was Miss Christian but was miserable inside. My expectations didn't match reality because I had heard well-meaning people say true Christians don't suffer from depression. Depression means a person has no hope, right? How is it possible to reconcile experiencing a hopeless existence while claiming to worship the God of hope?

Depression is deceptive. While it throbs with intensity inside the mind, it can appear like a tranquil lake on the outside. It can haunt the smiling cheerleader, the teacher, the mother, the pastor, or the successful business owner.

It demands energy you don't have. It leaves you overwhelmed. It tells you to hide. It attacks you with an ever-growing list of *shoulds*. It engulfs us in shame. "If I love God so much, why do I feel so apathetic? Why can't I find joy? What's wrong with me?"

Depression is the yawning chasm of darkness. Sometimes it's the result of the brokenness of a past that has never been dealt with, a trauma never healed. It can result from stress of an unexpected life event or exhaustion from pushing ourselves to the limit. Sometimes, depression just is. There's no rhyme or reason for it. A broken body in a broken world.

The pressure from trying to do it all left me unable to breathe, paralyzed in fear. As I lay sobbing on the bathroom floor, I remember saying, "God, I can't breathe. I'm drowning. This isn't the victorious life I was promised. Get me out of this. I don't care how."

Depression is a landmine that keeps on exploding. It leaves its victim a shell of the person they once were. It batters our emotions into numbness and tells us God either isn't there or doesn't care. It feels like a world of gray—a world without hope.

THE BLUEBIRD

Every morning, I walk outside to see my husband's driver's side mirror battered and smeared, evidence of another early morning fight.

When the sun rises each day, a male bluebird perches in front of my husband's rearview mirror and sees *himself*. But he thinks it's another male bluebird, just like him, and considers that bird a threat. A threat to his mate and to his babies. So, he does what must be done. He pecks the foul fowl until his head is nearly battered flat and his beak resembles the blunt end of a hammer. He doesn't realize he's fighting his own reflection. He's his own worst enemy.

I'm my own worst enemy too.

Our emotions often lie to us. Sometimes we believe if we *feel* a certain way, it must be so. We feel hopeless in our circumstances, so therefore there must not be hope. We experience a downturn in our circumstances or fortune, so therefore God does not love us.

Something *feels* real, so therefore it must *be* real.

Emotions are not good or bad. They just *are*. They are God-given ways of experiencing life in a profound way. The problem is our emotions are prone to violent swings based on mood, fatigue, perception, and a host of other issues.

At times, our emotions have very little to do with reality. They swing and dive with alarming speed. Truth doesn't.

Depression tells us there is no hope. That the way we feel now will be the way we'll feel forever. But it simply isn't true.

My own day-to-day roller coaster rides are proof of how quickly feelings can change. When I wake up, I'm usually tired and think, "Ugh. I don't want to get up." (Mood dive-bombs immediately.) Then after I slog into the kitchen, I find caffeine. (Mood improves.) I look at my annoying to-do list. (Mood disintegrates.) I see my children put their cereal bowls in the sink instead of leaving it in some other place. (Mood improves.) Then I hear screeching. "Mom, Nate just flushed his toy down the toilet, and it's overflowing!" (Mood is destroyed.)

See what I mean?

I can't be trusted to count on my own emotions any more than I should be considered as a nominee for a Nobel Prize.

When I'm threatening to drown in those suffocating, overwhelming crush of emotions, there is one place I can go that never changes. One sure foundation: the Word of God. Half of the battle is learning to believe what God says. To stop depending on my emotions as my compass. To trust that He is good and will do what He says He will do, despite how I feel or how hopeless things might look at the moment.

That's one of the biggest problems with depression: it tells you things will never get better. That you'll be numb forever. But just because something feels permanent doesn't mean it is.

DENIAL

When my doctor diagnosed me with depression in 2002, I almost did a spit-take. Me? Miss Has-It-Together-Preacher's-Kid? Not possible. But I couldn't escape the fact that something was wrong. Reality was at war with everything I had been taught and understood about the Christian life for years. If you love and trust Jesus, you will live victoriously, right?

Kind of.

Victorious over death—yes. Jesus gives us many victories and, of course, the ultimate is His victory over the grave. But He never promised we wouldn't go through some hard things. We live in a fallen world with fallen, frail bodies. The touch of sin is everywhere, and we will have to deal with it until He returns. In fact, Jesus actually said we would go through tough days and difficult seasons, but He promised to be there for us no matter what comes.

"I have told you these things, so that in me you may have peace. In this world you will have trouble. But take heart! I have overcome the world." (John 16:33, NIV)

In the meantime, we have to deal with death, disease, cancer, bad eyesight, bad hearts, diabetes, and, yes, even depression.

I fell into the mentality that says, "If you're depressed, you aren't close to Jesus. You don't love Him enough." How wrong I was.

We have the perfect example in King David.

From shepherd boy and underdog to champion, soldier, and refugee; from scorned and rejected to celebrated king, David's life is a study in stress. He left us a journal of his thoughts, struggles, tears, and victories in the Psalms.

Give me relief from my distress. Psalm 4:1, NIV

Heal me, LORD, for my bones are in agony.
My soul is in anguish. How long, LORD, how long? . . .
I am worn out from my groaning.
All night long I flood my bed with weeping
and drench my couch with tears. Psalm 6:2–3, 6, NIV

How long, LORD? Will you forget me forever?
How long will you hide Your face from me?
How long must I wrestle with my thoughts
and day after day have sorrow in my heart? Psalm 13:1–2, NIV

The cords of death entangled me;
the torrents of destruction overwhelmed me.
The cords of the grave coiled around me;
the snares of death confronted me. Psalm 18:4–5, NIV

Yet look at what David penned following these moments of torment:

In peace I will lie down and sleep,
For you alone, Lord,
make me dwell in safety. Psalm 4:8, NIV

The LORD has heard my cry for mercy. Psalm 6:9, NIV

I trust in your unfailing love;
my heart rejoices in your salvation. Psalm 13:5, NIV

In my distress I called to the LORD; . . .
From his temple he heard my voice; . . .
he drew me out of deep waters. Psalm 18:6, 16, NIV

The question isn't whether David should or should not have been depressed. We feel what we feel. But what is important is who he cried to for help. The Lord of lords, King of kings,

Creator, Jehovah. God called David a man after His own heart—not because he always had it together and did everything right but because David continually turned to the Lord in moments of joy and in despair.

Besides David, we have other examples of believers who battled depression, anxiety, and more. The famed evangelist Charles Spurgeon struggled mightily with these issues because of post-traumatic stress, health issues, and the loss of his grandchild. Spurgeon found depression would hit him with such ferocity that he would leave his home in London for long stretches of time in an attempt to lighten his dark moods. He said, "I could readily enough have laid violent hands upon myself, to escape from my misery of spirit."[9]

I've been there.

Desperation even drove Spurgeon to understand *why* so many of God's children struggle with dark moods and depression. In his writings, he concludes that if we want to be like Christ, we must share in His experiences. It's unlikely we'll be molded into His image if we enjoy a life of ease when He endured so much pain. "Do you expect to be crowned with gold where he was crowned with thorns? Shall lilies grow for you and briars for him?"[10] He considered the suffering of his depressive disorder a mark of being made more Christlike.

First Peter 1:6–7 (NLT) states, "There is wonderful joy ahead, even though you must endure many trials for a little while. These trials will show that your faith is genuine. It is being tested as fire tests and purifies gold—though your faith is far more precious than mere gold. So when your faith remains strong through many trials, it will bring you much praise and glory and honor on the day when Jesus Christ is revealed to the whole world."

This all sounds great, but I'll be honest: when my depression was at its worst, the last thing I cared about was the big picture. I just wanted the pain to stop.

That's normal. Going back to those pesky emotions we all battle, sometimes we may think that suffering must mean God is against us, that He no longer cares. But nothing could be further from the truth. Again, just because we feel something doesn't mean it's true.

DECEMBER SONGBIRD

I stared at the pregnancy test, my heart pounding.

Positive.

After the worst year of my married life—a year marked with financial strain, illness, and emotional turmoil—the tide was beginning to turn. It felt strange to be so happy. But perhaps God was moving us into a better place. The baby became our symbol of God's goodness, of hope.

Weeks into my pregnancy, I hemorrhaged. My husband rushed me to the hospital, and, after a night in the ER and several tests, the doctor came in, shaking her head.

"I'm sorry. Your baby is gone."

I was numb. Buzzing filled my ears. I tasted salt. My husband and I walked out of the ER, but I felt alone. Abandoned.

Sleep never came that night. I cried, alternating between disbelief and pain. I watched as the first streaks of sun painted the night sky. And that's when I heard it: a solitary bird singing its heart out. Where I live, birds don't chirp in winter. It's too miserable. Yet it refused to be quiet.

I rose from bed and walked to the window. My breath fogged the cold glass. As I stood there, empty and vulnerable,

I realized the songbird was making a choice. Despite the cold, despite what the rest of nature was doing, that little bird chose to rise from its bed and sing.

I faced a choice as well. I could either blame God and let bitterness consume me, or I could praise Him for the weeks that He gave me nurturing His creation. Praise Him that because of Jesus, I would see my child again.

Quoting the words of Job 1:21 (NKJV), I murmured, "The LORD gave and the LORD has taken away; Blessed be the name of the LORD." In that moment, a warmth enveloped me in a way that is hard to describe. It wasn't physical but spiritual. Supernatural. Somehow, I knew I wasn't abandoned. God was there.

Imagine my surprise, six months later, to discover I was expecting again. I was a little more cautious this time. Hopeful but not overjoyed. But the baby kept growing, my heart flooded with hope, and I thought maybe this was our reward for persevering.

When my baby was five months along, I miscarried again.

For weeks I groped through an emotional haze, barely managing day-to-day activities. I was numb. The world was gray. Worse still, I didn't sense God's presence with me at all. I continued to praise Him, just as I'd done when I lost the baby months before, but this was different. It was as if there was a yawning chasm between us. Spiritually, I resembled a blind woman groping through a strange room, hands extended, desperate for one touch from Him, any meager warmth, any sound or sigh or assurance. But I felt nothing.

I wondered if I had sinned in some horrid way that I was not even aware of. Why wouldn't God speak to me like He had before? I pleaded and begged and cried, and slowly over the span of months, the shroud lifted. It was so slow, so incremental, I almost missed it until I looked back. Although He had been silent, He was there.

How do I know that? Because I'm alive. I didn't give in to the darkness. He gave me the strength I needed each morning to rise from bed. He provided the next breath when I didn't believe I could breathe again. And here I stand today. Hopeful. Trusting. Steady.

Although the experience was miles apart from how I felt when I lost my first pregnancy, this second encounter with God was no less profound. I wonder if He didn't reveal His presence immediately because it forced me to seek Him with greater ferocity. Every fiber of my being yearned for Him, and the tears, prayers, and lamentations of those dark months were like a guidepost on my journey with Him. It was a marker I didn't even understand until I looked back to see how far He'd led me.

We are creatures who often want God to take us out of our situation, but He knows the struggle is what will mold us into His image and draw our hearts to His closer over time.

BLESSED

From His Sermon on the Mount (Matthew 5–7), Jesus said the blessed were those who mourned, the meek, the merciful, the pure in heart, the peacemakers, and the persecuted. Nothing about personal happiness or financial success in there. You won't find any verses about God's will for His children to climb the ladder of accomplishments or to be comfortable.

God is not nearly so concerned with our happiness, or even getting us out of our current circumstances, as He is in transforming us into the image of His Son *through* our circumstances. His goal is His glory for His great Name and our good.

Please don't misunderstand me. I'm not saying God wants us to suffer. He doesn't glory in our pain. What I'm saying is that He can use it to bring us to a new place of understanding, of growth, and yes, even joy.

BUT WHY?

Why depression? What causes it?

I wish there were a simple answer. A simple answer would mean a simple solution. The reasons vary from person to person and often take many years to figure out. Depression is usually highly complex and multifaceted. Physical, emotional, and environmental issues can all play a part. Sometimes, it can be hard to find any explanation for depression.

That's why it's so important to avoid equating mood with spirituality. Depression doesn't mean you're a terrible Christian. It means something physical, psychological, or spiritual is out of step and needs to be addressed.

It took me a long time of healing, counseling, and rest, but after a lengthy recovery and healing process, I eventually became thankful for that horrid season of depression. Why? Because God used it to catch my attention.

I had exhausted myself trying to keep people happy, attempting to earn their love. I couldn't. It left me exhausted and disillusioned. I learned being busy *for* God is not the same as being close *to* God. I'm not sure anything would have changed had God not used depression as the impetus to transform my life from the inside out.

Whether the cause of depression is a result of abuse, genetics, people-pleasing, trauma, hormones, or a host of other reasons, shame should not be part of the attempted solution.

Depression is just as physical as it is emotional and spiritual. Would we dare accuse a person with bad eyesight of "not trusting God" for wearing glasses before slipping behind the driver's wheel? Do we shun and disparage the diabetic for taking insulin? Or the heart patient for using beta blockers? Depression is no different.

Sometimes it seems like people have less of a problem with a Christian being depressed than they do when a Christian takes medication for their depression.

THE LITTLE WHITE PILL

Some days I loathe it. Other days I nearly weep with gratitude for it. Strange dichotomy.

Every time I look at that little white pill in my palm, I am overcome with an odd mix of emotions. When I was diagnosed with depression in 2002, I was desperate for relief from the dark shroud that had blanketed my mind and heart.

But I balked when my doctor suggested medication to ease my physical symptoms. I was a Christian. Wasn't medication a sign of weakness for a girl who claims to trust God? Perhaps I was still in denial. Maybe taking a pill would make the diagnosis much more real than I cared to admit. Confusion battered my mind and heart. I had heard well-meaning believers condemning others who sought medical help for their depression, throwing out their careless barbs and accusations with frightening speed.

"You should trust God more."

"You shouldn't get down."

"If you'll read this scripture, you should feel better."

All those *shoulds* and *shouldn'ts* wreaked havoc with my peace of mind. That is, until God revealed this beautiful truth to my heart: grace is greater than all the times I fall short of the *shoulds*. I'm a mess but I don't have to pretend to be something other than who I am. God knew I would fail in and of myself. That's why He sent a Savior.

Do I believe in gobbling down pills as the end all and be all? No, absolutely not. Taking medication allows me to deal with the physical symptoms as I lean on the Holy Spirit to reveal any emotional or spiritual issues that have become roots of trouble. And for some, there *is* no discernible cause for their depression. Bodies just don't work like they are supposed to. We are living in a broken world with frail bodies. Eyesight fails. Thyroid levels fluctuate. Skin loses its elasticity. And yes, even Christians can get depressed.

Speaking for myself, I'm glad I listened and took the medication. My husband and children need me at my best, not a mere shadow of myself. It was a God-given tool to help ease physical symptoms and replenish my body of the chemicals it needed so I could focus on the work of discovering *why* I was depressed. Thanks to God's gentle love, He tenderly revealed the wounds I carried inside and healed me in profound ways. He's still healing me.

Fast forward to the present. I am in a much better place these days. My walk with God is vibrant. I know the warning signs of depression and have a proactive plan in place to combat the cycles that once pulled me down. So why can't I function without that little white pill?

Last week, as I was bemoaning my dependency on it, I cried out to God in frustration. "Why? Why do I still need this? Why can't I live and laugh without it? Must I forever carry the scars of 2002 with me?"

He spoke to me swiftly, His voice a gentle whisper as He impressed this thought into my heart: *What if you no longer needed this medicine? Would you forget? Would you forget what I've brought you through? Would you forget what that black place feels like? Would you be able to help others struggling with the same issues if your heart grows numb to the pain you once suffered? I have brought you this far. I've walked you through every valley. This reminder keeps you from repeating the mistakes you once made, living to please people instead of seeking my heart. My grace is sufficient for you. My strength is made perfect in your weakness.*

I'm trying not to look at that little white pill as a chain any longer. It's a tool, a reminder of the compassionate way He led me through the darkness to find hope and joy in Him again. Kind of like Jonah and his fish. Being swallowed by a fish wasn't Jonah's punishment for running away. No, that fish was grace. From the dark, sour confines of its belly, God captured Jonah's attention and redirected his life into victory. Depression was my fish of grace.

Accusations of "a lack of faith," or simply sharing a scripture in hopes that the afflicted person will soon bounce back from a blue funk, often cause someone battling depression to recoil deeper into isolation.

The solution is not that simple.

Deep-seated emotional issues are not created overnight, nor can they be healed overnight. We have become a people uncomfortable with the messy. We don't like what we don't understand, so we try to force it into a box, put a bow on it and say, "Jesus will heal it. Smile and let's praise Him." Meanwhile, those who are hurting know the wounds have not been cleaned or healed, merely bandaged over. And suggesting easy solutions can cause the depressed to feel more isolated and alone than ever before.

There's a better way to handle depression than pretending we don't experience it, or that if we offer a verse here and there, the suffering will disappear. God showed us exactly how to address depression in the story of Elijah.

STILL SMALL VOICE

Elijah had just led an awe-inspiring victory over the prophets of Baal and Asherah in front of the entire nation of Israel. But when Elijah heard Queen Jezebel wanted to kill him, he panicked and ran (1 Kings 18). After a terror-filled flight to Beersheba, Elijah sent his servant away and collapsed in the wilderness. Unfortunately for Elijah, depression feeds on isolation. And isolation, along with mental, spiritual, and physical fatigue, leads to disaster.

> *He came to a broom bush, sat down under it and prayed that he might die. "I have had enough,* Lord*," he said. "Take my life; I am no better than my ancestors." Then he lay down under the bush and fell asleep.* 1 Kings 19:4–5, NIV

Elijah was ready to die. He wanted out. Oh, how I've been there. I just wanted the pain and the overwhelming fatigue to stop.

God could have told Elijah to get his act together, to remember scriptures, to pray harder, or have more faith, but He didn't. God provided for Elijah in much more loving ways.

> *All at once an angel touched him and said, "Get up and eat." He looked around, and there by his head was some bread baked over hot coals, and a jar of water. He ate and drank and then lay down again. The angel of the* Lord *came back a second time and touched him and said, "Get up and eat, for the journey is too much for you." So he got up and ate and drank.* 1 Kings 19:5–8, NIV

God didn't condemn or shame Elijah into healing. He first sent an angel so Elijah wouldn't be alone, tending to his emotional needs. God then took care of Elijah's physical needs, like food, water, and sleep. We can't correctly address spiritual needs until the first two have been met. After Elijah had recovered physically, then God was able to reveal the spiritual issue needing to be addressed.

> *Then a great and powerful wind tore the mountains apart and shattered the rocks before the LORD, but the LORD was not in the wind. After the wind there was an earthquake, but the LORD was not in the earthquake. After the earthquake came a fire, but the LORD was not in the fire. And after the fire came a gentle whisper.* 1 Kings 19:11–12, NIV

Depression might feel like a powerful wind, an earthquake, or a fire—loud, destructive, terrifying—but God has no part in those things.

> *When Elijah heard it, he pulled his cloak over his face and went out and stood at the mouth of the cave. Then a voice said to him, "What are you doing here, Elijah?" He replied, "I have been very zealous for the LORD God Almighty. The Israelites have rejected your covenant, torn down your altars, and put your prophets to death with the sword. I am the only one left, and now they are trying to kill me too." The LORD said to him . . . "I reserve seven thousand in Israel—all whose knees have not bowed down to Baal and whose mouths have not kissed him."* 1 Kings 19:13–18, NIV

God didn't rake Elijah over the proverbial coals but gently reminded him, "You are not alone." He nurtured him into healing.

That's what we need. To know we aren't alone. To know that our condition won't be our conclusion. To find hope. To sense God's presence with us when everything else is numb and gray.

Depression is a liar, but it doesn't come to stay.

FROM DARKNESS TO LIGHT

Through my season of darkness, I learned that God is tender. He cradled me in the midst of that difficult time, stayed with me when I felt alone, restored my heart, and transformed my spiritual walk. It wasn't easy. I needed medical help. I needed to unlearn and replace harmful thought patterns. I needed time. I needed grace.

God gave it in abundance. He also provided sweet people along the journey who had experienced the same thing. Their encouragement was a lifeline. I had no idea so many believers struggled with depression, but they do—far more than I realized.

I don't have all the answers. I only know we must do better supporting one another. Listening more than we speak. Making sure we take time to rest, turn off our phones, and have safe places to share our messy stuff without condemnation.

Most of all, we should pray. Pray for sensitivity. Pray for our eyes to be opened to those silently suffering. If we see another struggling under the weight of their load, we offer a helping hand. Galatians 6:2 (NLT) tells us this: "Share each other's burdens, and in this way obey the law of Christ." For all the uncertainties, lack of answers, and complexities, there was one abiding truth I learned in the darkness: God is there.

Amen.

BIBLE VERSE

Even when I walk through the darkest valley, I will not be afraid, for you are close beside me. Your rod and your staff protect and comfort me. (Psalm 23:4, NLT)

READER TAKEAWAY

Depression is a lie that tells us God either isn't with us or doesn't care about our suffering. If we believe these lies, we will be left despondent and doubting God's goodness.

THE TRUTH

Even though we may not always sense God with us, He is. He is with us in the darkness and uses every difficult experience to mold us into His image.

QUESTION

In what ways do your emotions lie to you? When you look back over your life, when has God been leading you, even if you didn't realize it at the time?

CHAPTER 6

The Lie of Insecurity

I could hear the fight from the trail below me as I climbed Pinnacle Mountain. Actually, *everyone* in the vicinity of the snaking path could hear the epic battle of wills between the frustrated father and his stubborn son on the crowded mountainside.

"Son, I mean it. Stop and tie your shoe."

"No, I don't want to."

"You're going to trip and get hurt."

Silence as the determined boy marched past his father.

"Ethan, I mean it. Stop right now and tie your shoe. It's an order."

"I won't!"

I peered up ahead, spying the arguing duo from my spot on the trail.

The father was so angry he nearly screamed. "Fine! If you fall and break your neck, it won't be on me!"

Little Ethan huffed. "I'd rather break my neck than stop and tie my shoes."

The father plunged his fingers into his own hair and yanked, his frustration mounting. "Why? Why on earth won't you just stop and tie your shoe?"

Little Ethan turned, a scowl on his freckled face. "If I stop, everyone around us will think I'm tired! That I'm a wimp! I'm not going to stop and let them think I'm not tough enough to climb up this mountain!"

The father scratched his head. "Maybe they'll just think you needed to tie your shoe."

Ethan shook his head. "No, it's not worth the risk. I'd rather fall than anyone think that I'm a wimp."

This is an example of rampant insecurity on display.

Insecurity makes us jealous. It makes us control freaks. It causes us to wallow in suspicion. Insecurity births braggarts, fits of temper, infidelity, a need for constant validation, or the inability to be happy unless everyone around us is happy. Its nagging voice makes us think the worst of others, assigning them motives that don't exist. In short, insecurity causes us to do the craziest, and sometimes, most harmful things imaginable. And not just to ourselves. It colors and stains every single relationship in our lives.

Boiled down to its most fundamental existence, insecurity is a lie that screams, "You're not good enough!" And if we believe the lie, it wreaks havoc in our hearts and lives.

CONDEMNED HEARTS

Close your eyes. Imagine you're staring at a condemned house. Weeds and ivy have taken over the land. Broken glass litters the ground. A window in front is boarded shut with splintered wood. The windows upstairs are broken and dark. The roof is caving in and the entire structure is in shambles. Everything about the house resembles death, darkness, danger, and broken dreams.

And across the front door, there is a sign that reads "Keep Out."

Some might view this scene as depressing. Others may find it intriguing or even a tad romantic. What could possibly have led to such a sad sight? What was the story behind the old house?

For me, the sight overwhelms me with sadness. It represents the death of dreams, of life, of light. A condemned house smacks of something precious that was slowly and painfully destroyed, whether intentionally or through neglect.

Do you know what is even more upsetting? Many of us have hung a condemned sign over our own hearts.

Our lives can often resemble condemned houses, and these usually take two different forms: the scare-away or the fake-out.

The scare-away house is in shambles. Signs are plastered all over it warning people of the imminent danger of approaching. In the same way, a scare-away heart means the person is so insecure that they live in fear. They dwell on their past mistakes. They are so terrified of opening themselves to others that they hang the "keep out" sign in front. They appear cranky and unlovable as a way to protect their hearts.

The second condemned house is the fake-out house. It's a little trickier to identify. It looks good on the outside. But the inside, oh mercy! It's structurally unsound. There are massive holes in the drywall. An engineer could come through and fill up an entire clipboard full of problems in every corner. However, the public and real estate agents may miss it because of the fresh paint covering the walls and the warm cookies on the counter.

The fake-out heart is little different from the scare-away heart except that it keeps its pain carefully hidden, coated in pretty paint and good works but broken inside. We run the PTA, we gather accomplishments and accolades, striving for the perfect life. But inside we are cracked and broken, wallowing in insecurity, keeping our fear and wounds safely hidden from prying eyes because "Fake it 'til you make it," right? I've never liked that saying.

Fake isn't authentic. If you're faking something, it's because you don't believe it. If you don't believe it, no one else will either. You might be able to cover up your wounds with a bit of spackle and fresh paint, but the truth eventually comes out.

Where does insecurity come from? Let's discuss several factors that make us feel "less than."

COMPARING OURSELVES TO OTHERS

I've noticed that when I compare myself to someone else, I always draw one of two comparisons. I either think, *Man, compared to this chick, my life looks amazing. She's a hot mess!* I puff up my own pride at the expense of another. The other option is to say, *Compared to her, I look awful. My family doesn't have nearly as much money as they do. Why did they get to go to Hawaii for vacation while I'm stuck at home with screaming kids and a stack of bills?* This comparison leads to feelings of shame and worthlessness.

Neither option is healthy.

In a perfect world, comparison wouldn't exist at all. We would celebrate one another, grieve with one another, and encourage one another with no traces of malice, fear, or insecurity.

Unfortunately, we don't live in a perfect world. And the biggest issue with insecurity in the life of the child of God is that it devalues a person He's made for a glorious purpose: *you*. Psalm 139:16 (NLT) reminds me that God "saw me before I was born.

Every day of my life was recorded in your book. Every moment was laid out before a single day had passed."

Before you ever took a breath, God had a distinct plan for your life, and that plan did not include having you pretend to be someone else or compare your worth to someone else's.

We have a beautiful example of this in the Indian fable of "The Cracked Pot":

Long ago there lived a man whose job it was to haul water from the stream uphill to his master's house many times each day. To do this work, the water bearer had two large pots that hung from each end of a pole he carried across the back of his neck, balanced over the top of his shoulders. The two pots were identical, but only one of them was perfect—the other one had a small crack in it, so with every trip up the hill the cracked pot lost nearly half of its water while the perfect pot delivered a full portion.

The perfect pot was proud of its accomplishments, and loved to brag about them. He also loved to point out to the cracked pot how flawed it was…that no matter how hard the water bearer worked, the cracked pot only ever managed to deliver a half portion of water to the master's house. The cracked pot felt ashamed of his imperfection and was miserable that he could accomplish only half of what he had been made to do.

One day, the cracked pot spoke to the water bearer when they had stopped by the stream. "I am ashamed of myself, and I must apologize to you for my flaw…for my inability to carry all the water you need me to carry. You work so hard and I fail to give you the full value for your effort."

The water bearer listened and looked upon the pot with compassion and said, "As we return to the master's house this time, I want you to pay attention to the beautiful flowers growing along the path." And indeed, as they went back up the hill, the cracked pot did take notice of the sun warming the beautiful wild flowers on the side of the path, and felt cheered...somewhat. But at the end of the trail, the pot again felt miserable and apologized once more for having lost half its water along the way.

The water bearer said to the pot, "I'm afraid you do not understand what I was trying to show you. Did you not notice that there were flowers only on your side of your path, and not on the other pot's side? That's because I planted flower seeds on your side of the path, and every day while we walk back from the stream, you've watered them. I have known about your crack for some time and could have crafted a new pot. But because of your flaw, we have been able...together... to grow beautiful flowers and with them bless many tables. Without you being just the way you are, where would we have found such beauty?[11]

Your flaws don't make you unusable or determine your worth. Instead, those broken places are the very things God can use to show His beauty and power in someone else's life.

There's no need to compare.

FINDING OUR WORTH OUTSIDE OF GOD

Security in any earthly thing will not last. If we try to fill our need to be loved or seen as significant by someone, something, or anyone other than Jesus, we will be disappointed.

If the pleasures of this world lasted, we wouldn't have to keep seeking and repeating them over and over and over again. They're false gods. Idols. Poisoned apples. And they will leave us empty every single time.

Sometimes, I fall into the "if I only had or was this thing" mentality. "If I was thinner, then my life would be better." "If I only had a bigger house, then I would be happier." "If I could receive that promotion at work, then everyone would respect me." If, if, if.

If your security relies on an *if*, it can't and won't make you happy in the long run. Anything in this world that we place on the throne of our hearts, including people, has the potential to fall, be broken, or crumble. I love what Corrie Ten Boom said one day while speaking to Charles Swindoll: "You must learn to hold everything loosely . . . everything. Even your dear family. Why? Because the Father may wish to take one of them back to Himself, and when He does, it will hurt you if He must pry your fingers loose."[12]

SUCCUMBING TO PRIDE

We're creatures that waffle between thinking we are the absolute best at something and then, when we find out someone is better, we fear we may actually be the worst. Our pendulum swings between inflated ego and self-loathing. Both are bad places to dwell.

Pride is the reason so many of us lie. We want to be included. Pride is the reason we claw our way to being noticed by someone, *anyone*. It puffs us up and makes us feel important—until someone comes along and directly or inadvertently exposes our flaws. Our fat balloon of self-importance deflates like a pancake.

EXPERIENCING JEALOUSY

Confidence is silent. Insecurity is loud, and never does it scream louder than when we're jealous.

We find the perfect example of this in the evil queen from *Snow White*. Trust me, I have had a lot of time to consider the story while reading it to my kids. The queen spent an inordinate amount of time looking at her reflection, chanting, "Looking glass upon the wall, who is the fairest of us all?" Her obsession with her beauty wrecked her entire life. As long as the mirror said, "You, my queen, are fairest of all," everything in her kingdom was calm. She was on top of the world, secure in her status as most beautiful . . . until the pedestal she erected for herself came crashing down.

"Looking-glass upon the wall, who is the fairest of us all?"

The mirror replied, Queen, you are very fair, 'tis true, but Snow White fairer is than you."

The queen was sick with jealousy, writhing hatred, and an insecurity that nearly rattled her insides apart.

We've all been there.

Our culture is obsessed with perfect bodies. They're plastered all over the magazines lining the racks of the grocery store, television, and social media. Whether it's about diets, workouts, skin imperfections or anything similar, people are always thinking about ways to try to look like a model. There are even slimming pants available that are infused with caffeine to help melt cellulite. Do what the experts say to attain physical perfection and the fulfillment of your dreams.

Too many of us look in the mirror to bask in our reflection until we scroll through social media, see everyone else's reel and it's like the magic mirror all over again. *Suzie has lost a lot of weight. She's been buying designer clothes and going to the gym, while I've been inhaling bags of cookies. Ugh. She makes me so angry, posting all those pics. She just needs attention.*

Jealousy strikes at more than just physical appearance. We can become jealous about anything and everything. It can be as simple as being passed over for an accolade at work or someone coming between people in a valued relationship. Insecurity breeds fear, suspicion, rage, and humiliation. And where these kinds of emotions live, love cannot exist.

CONDEMNATION DEFINED

Let's look back at those condemned houses I mentioned before. *Condemned* has several definitions, including "pronounced guilty and sentenced to punishment" and "officially declared to be unfit for use."

How often do we condemn ourselves with insecurity? We tell ourselves that we will never be good enough, that we are guilty of something God has forgiven us for but for which we can't forgive ourselves. And we say unkind things to ourselves.

I'm pathetic.

I'm useless.

How could God truly love me? I'm not good enough.

Compared to ________________, I'm terrible.

Whether we realize it or not, this negative self-talk can be one of the subtle forms of condemnation. And when a house is condemned, what happens? It's no longer habitable and is scheduled for destruction.

Many of us confuse conviction with condemnation. So what's the difference between the two? I believe it comes down to the purpose.

Let's make a list to contrast them.

Condemnation	**Conviction**
Comes from self/others	Comes from Holy Spirit
Intends to tear you down	Intends to lift up and set free
Focuses on self	Focuses on God

Points out failures	Points out hope and forgiveness
Avoids the solution	Jesus invites you to come to Him
Guilt and shame	Godly sorrow to lead to repentance

Simply put, condemnation points out all your flaws, but conviction exposes the truth in love. God will never tell you that you're a loser.

Oftentimes, we heap guilt and expectations on ourselves, for no other reason than simply being a broken human. We compare ourselves to others, live in the world of *should*, only to realize we can never measure up. Even more destructive, we inadvertently blame God because we have no idea how He could possibly love us unconditionally.

I think sometimes we focus more on what we *hear* about God, than what we really know about Him. The world seems to have this idea that God is constantly frowning, pointing a finger at His children, demanding we do the perfection dance to win His good graces. Nothing could be further from the truth. If you have given your life to Christ and accepted His gift of love and redemption, you are no longer condemned in His eyes. Romans 8:1 (NLT) tells us this: "There is no condemnation for those who belong to Christ Jesus." We belong to Him.

God doesn't want you to feel condemned, broken, or useless. In fact, His Son died so you wouldn't feel that way any longer. When we grasp how deeply He loves us, it changes the way we view ourselves.

It's a Wonderful Life is one of my favorite movies. George Bailey is continually baffled by the beauty his wife sees in their old, drafty, worn-down home. He only sees the creaking steps and sagging trim. But Mary Bailey's eyes light up with hope and promise when she views their big, rambling house. She sees the hidden beauty just waiting to be exposed. And I believe that is exactly how God sees us.

It's time to know and rely on the unconditional, overwhelming love God has for us. Sometimes our insecurities scream that we'll never be good enough, or smart enough, or brave enough. But the truth is we don't have to be. Jesus is all of those things for us.

And every time you're tempted to hang up the "Condemned" sign, remember that your name is engraved on the palm of His hands (Isaiah 49:16). You're no longer condemned.

EL ROI

The lie of insecurity tells us we're not good enough. That we're lacking and worth less than everyone around us. The natural reaction then is to either puff up our own ego to fill that void or cower in shame. When we think our value is negligible, we settle for being overlooked, unheard, and unseen.

One of my favorite names for God is *El Roi*, meaning "The God who sees me." A lowly slave girl discovered this firsthand.

> *Sarai treated Hagar so harshly that she finally ran away. The angel of the* Lord *found Hagar beside a spring of water in the wilderness, along the road to Shur. The angel said to her, "Hagar, Sarai's servant, where have you come from, and where are you going?"*
>
> *"I'm running away from my mistress, Sarai," she replied.*
>
> *The angel of the* Lord *said to her, "Return to your mistress, and submit to her authority." Then he added, "I will give you more descendants than you can count."*
>
> *And the angel also said, "You are now pregnant and will give birth to a son. You are to name him Ishmael (which means 'God hears'), for the* Lord *has heard your cry of distress." . . . Thereafter, Hagar used another name to refer to*

> *the LORD, who had spoken to her. She said, "You are the God who sees me."* Genesis 16:6–11, 13 NLT

If anyone had reason to be insecure, it was Hagar. She was enslaved, abused, and without anywhere to turn. Yet despite her circumstances, God saw her. He heard. And He raised her up to be mother of a brand-new people.

We all want to be seen, to know that we matter. In the presence of Jesus, there is no need to hide. No need to wallow in the dark pain of insecurity. No need to drop our gazes in shame. He sees. He knows, yet He loves us all the same.

If I am to be seen, I want it to be through His love-filled eyes. Eyes that see the blood of His Son marked upon my heart. Eyes that saw my faults yet loved me so much He would have rather died than leave me in the dark.

LABELS AND WORTH

It doesn't matter whether I'm in a church full of women or at a prison filled with inmates; when I'm teaching about the lies I have believed, innumerable women tell me they fell for the lie "I'm worthless." When I ask who else has struggled with this, every hand in the room goes up. Why?

After listening to story after story, one common denominator seems to resonate through most of these women's issues: someone at some point gave them a label that stuck, and that label birthed rabid insecurity.

I recently conducted a social media poll asking my friends what their nicknames were growing up. Some of my favorites were Snicklefritz, Squeaky, Casper, Noodle, Idget, and Sassafras. Cute. Sweet. Then things took a turn. People also shared nicknames that were hurtful: Tubby, Fatso, or Motor Mouth, to name a few. Names can turn into labels. Labels stick. Soon we begin to believe the lie that we are what the label advertises.

To put it another way, labels usually tell us what's inside, right? If I walk into my pantry and grab a can that bears a label showing plump, juicy peaches, I don't expect to open the can and find black-eyed peas inside. The label system works great for canned foods and organizing closets but not for defining our own worth.

Some of us are slapped with a label just once, maybe twice, by some cruel person, and we believe the lie. We mistakenly believe we are what the label advertises.

Maybe you have a label stuck to you that refuses to come off. Maybe it's Unwanted, Unlovable, Problem Child, Black Sheep, Depressed, Divorced, Loser, or Never Good Enough.

You are more than the label someone has given you.

Insecurity is often birthed in rejection. You might have lived through the slicing pain of divorce. A nasty breakup. Perhaps you've been mistreated by your family, mistreated by your coworkers, or fired from your job. You might be dealing with the mess from your own consequences and poor decisions, and you just need a little grace from people unwilling to give it.

When wrestling with the crippling lie of insecurity, we must cling to the truth that our worth doesn't come from what we do, what we own, how we look, or any other external factor. Our value is firmly rooted in grasping the knowledge that we are loved and cherished by our Creator. Each of us needs to take hold of this and let it sink into our minds and hearts. When we believe it with every part of our being, our confidence becomes unshakable. The perception of our worth would not change based on someone's ability to see it.

Consider a priceless work of art like Van Gogh's *Starry Night*. Pretend you are walking down the street when suddenly you are stunned to see the painting carelessly tossed into a dumpster. Why would anyone do such a thing? Clearly the owner had no idea of its value.

Did the painting's worth change based on its location or who owned it? No. Its value remained the same. This scenario only shows us the ignorance of the person who discarded it.

We should never allow someone who doesn't understand our value to define our worth.

BARNEYS IN A *GQ* WORLD

I adore Barney Fife from *The Andy Griffith Show*. He's such a lovable mix of insecurity, overconfidence, and legalism. It's a kick to hear him espouse his vast wisdom and then see him fall flat on his face.

Ultimately, people like Barney battle one main enemy: insecurity. They are not confident about who they are, so they overcompensate by acting invincible. I think of Yosemite Sam from Looney Tunes, whose mix of low self-esteem and too much power is a dangerous combination.

Self-esteem is a buzz word these days. We worry about our children's self-esteem. We compare ourselves to others, wallowing in jealousy when they accomplish something we've only dreamed of. We think we can fix our insecurities by trying to be like the people we see in glossy magazines like *GQ*. We measure our worth based on our accomplishments, our looks, our financial security, and our popularity.

Every single one of these hole-fillers will pass away. They will not last. My personal opinion is that we need a shift from self-esteem to self-respect and God-worth.

Self-esteem is like looking at yourself in a small mirror. The only thing you can really see is your own reflection. However, self-respect is like looking at your reflection from a large window. You can see your image, but you can also see the image and environment of everyone around you.

This is a subtle but important difference. Self-respect is unselfish. It's remembering that this life is not about me or about you. It's all about Christ and His kingdom.

Speaking for myself, when insecurity strikes, my pride takes a beating, so I feel the need to puff it back up. I try to justify myself and rationalize my decisions to make myself feel better. But the Bible says even my very best is like filthy rags. Held up next to God's glory, I am dirty, dingy, messy.

My worth is not determined by how good I am, what I do, or what I accomplish. True worth is found in a relationship with Christ. Knowing that the God of the universe, the same God who carved out the oceans, created you, that He draws you to Him, and that He has your days planned before you are even one day old is an amazing thought.

Yes, some of us are Barneys in a *GQ* world. And you know what? That's OK. *GQ* will pass away. The world will pass away. But Jesus remains.

GOD-WORTH

It's time we trade in the lie of insecurity and replace it with God-worth.

God-worth is knowing who we belong to. It's grasping hold of the truth that Jesus thought you were so valuable, He went to the farthest lengths possible to save you. He would have rather died than leave you in the dark.

That is true love. And it makes each of us more precious than all the silver and gold the world can hold.

Insecurity screams, "I'm not as good as __________." But having a healthy God-worth says, "Another person's talents does not erase my own."

Insecurity shouts, "I have to be perfect or no one will accept me." God-worth whispers, "God's unconditional love for me never wavers, whether I'm at my best or scraping bottom at my worst."

Let's return to the example of Snow White. I'm a homeschooling mom, and I recently gave my two girls an interesting writing assignment. "I want you to tell me what you would see if your mirror reflected what you looked like on the inside instead of the outside."

My oldest definitely doesn't feel insecure. In fact, she went the other direction—diva mode. She wrote, "If I looked in the mirror and saw inside of me instead of outside, I would see kindness, joy, a girly-girl who is loving and popular. The advantage is that I get to see who I am today, but the disadvantage is that I want to see my pretty face."

Can you see me rolling my eyes? I'm convinced she writes stuff like this solely to aggravate me. With my trusty red pen, I wrote under her paragraph, "You might see pride as well."

My youngest daughter, however, wrote something very interesting. She penned, "If my mirror showed my inside instead of my outside, the picture in the mirror would be beautiful because Jesus saved me. It would be His face I would see in the mirror."

She nailed it.

Our job is not to ask a magic mirror for our worth. Instead, we are to *be* the mirror. Our purpose is to reflect Jesus.

There's something we can do instead of gazing into our mirrors each morning and chanting, "Looking-glass upon the wall, who is the fairest of us all?" We should rise and pray, "Looking-glass upon the wall, I want to see Jesus living inside of me."

THE WOUND

Crushing the lie of insecurity is twofold. First, we must learn to see ourselves the way God does.

God created each of us with a beautiful purpose in mind. Psalm 139 tells us this:

> *You created my inmost being; you knit me together in my mother's womb. I praise you because I am fearfully and wonderfully made; your works are wonderful, I know that full well. My frame was not hidden from you when I was made in the secret place, when I was woven together in the depths of the earth. Your eyes saw my unformed body; all the days ordained for me were written in your book before one of them came to be.* Psalm 139:13–16, NIV

God calls us His children (1 John 3:1) and loved us so much that He died to redeem us (Romans 5:8). Since He was willing to give up His life for ours, we are more valuable than all the treasures of the universe.

Once we understand our value, we need to be brave enough to be honest about our wounds.

Not long ago, my two-year-old son fell outside on the driveway and scraped up his hand. At the sound of his wailing, his sisters and I ran to his side. When the girls tried to convince him to let them see, he covered the scrape with his chubby fingers and jerked away from them with a teary scowl. Why? Because he didn't trust them with his boo-boo. He'd been the victim of their teasing enough to wonder if they were trustworthy. Would they tease him? Laugh at him for being melodramatic? Unintentionally make the hurt worse by poking and probing? No, letting them see was too risky.

I've been there. I've made the mistake of showing my hard things to people unable to help and their attempts to do so only caused more pain.

What do we do with a wound? Usually, we try to hide it.

When I approached my son and knelt down in front of him with sympathy, he finally uncovered his injured hand to let me examine the damage. He trusted me not to hurt him any more than he'd already been wounded.

Here's the thing—there was no way for me to give him the help he needed until I could understand how severe his injury was. Once he was brave enough to lift his little fingers away from his wound, I could treat it. Because he trusted me, I was able to wash it, clean it with hydrogen peroxide, bandage it, and kiss it until his tears subsided and he was playing once more.

This is a beautiful parallel to what happens in our own lives. Because we live as messy people in a broken world, we all have wounds. Some are bigger than others. Some have cuts deeper than others. Some of us have lived with the crippling shame of sexual, verbal, or physical abuse. Some of us have been told we're unwanted or unloved. Some of us can't seem to shake depression or are mourning the loss of a loved one. Some of us have a childhood that we barely survived or an adulthood that has left us disillusioned and depressed. Some of us are victims of our own horrible mistakes.

And the same way my son covered his scraped palm, we cover our hurt, wrapping our fingers around the searing pain, keeping it concealed, restrained, and locked away from prying eyes. We don't want anyone to see, anyone to know. The pain is too deep, the vulnerability too precarious—that is, until someone unintentionally pokes at us and all of our insecurities and pain flare back to life.

This is the crux of the matter when it comes to insecurity; God can't heal what we are unwilling to expose to Him. When we are brave enough to come to Him with all of our shame and broken pieces, His light and love can start to heal those nasty wounds. He is our safe place. A Father who lovingly cleans the wound and kisses the sting away.

What happens with a deep wound when it finally heals? It leaves a scar. Scars tell a story. They are proof that you were hurt and survived. *Living* from your scars gives hope to others who are hurting, those who are still trying to hide their devastating wound from curious eyes.

Be brave. Be courageous. Live from your scars. There is a world of hurting people needing to see that wounds can be healed by the Great Physician, and it's the perfect way to silence the lies of insecurity.

BIBLE VERSE

There is no condemnation for those who belong to Christ Jesus. (Romans 8:1, NLT)

READER TAKEAWAY

Insecurity is a result of not embracing our worth in Christ and hiding our wounds from the One who can heal them. A sure sign of its presence is jealousy, and it can cause us to live a life of condemning emotions and behaviors.

THE TRUTH

Jesus loved you so much, He died to save you. Our worth is not in what we do or how we look but by what He has done for us.

QUESTION

How would your life be different if you were able to lay down insecurity?

CHAPTER 7

The Lie of Willpower

The "Stop It" sketch starring Bob Newhart on *Mad TV* is a classic, both for its humor and for its truth.[13]

Let me give you a quick rundown: Bob Newhart is playing a therapist, and a woman enters his office as a new patient. He tells her he only charges five dollars for a five-minute session. She is baffled but pleased. How often can you get a deal like that?

He listens as she confesses her terrifying phobia of being buried alive in a box, a debilitating neurosis that has left her in a cycle of paralyzing fear. After nodding, he tells her he has two words that will change her life. She eagerly grabs her pencil and paper to write down his advice. She watches him carefully, ready to absorb his wisdom. After a pause, he leans in and yells, "Stop it!" The woman is dumbstruck.

With every phobia or fear she confesses his answer is always the same: "Stop it!" In the end—fearing he can't get through to her because of her frustration with his therapy advice—he yells, "Stop it or I'll bury you alive in a box!"

Although the skit had me laughing, I confess feeling a niggling sense of unease as I watched it. Why? Because I fear this is how many of us handle our problems.

Whatever our past abuse or trauma, no matter the circumstances or crushing blows, too often we demand this sudden halt from ourselves and others. "Stop it!" "Don't do that." "Do what's right and stop doing what's wrong." So we think if we work a little harder, by sheer force of our own will we'll finally defeat our demons, whether they be food, overspending, drug or alcohol addiction, gossiping, exercise, and everything in between. We download apps to help us manage our time, our calories, or our budget. We adhere to stricter schedules. We set ourselves up for success in every possible way, and it works for a little while. And then?

We fall.

The lie of willpower says we can achieve anything, do anything through our own ability. That we can accomplish the impossible through our own strength. The problem is we usually leave God out of the equation. We become our own god and are crushed when our intentions and resolutions come crashing down.

SAME OLD STORY

I did it again.

After years of battling approval addiction, after years teaching others how to break free from the chains of people-pleasing, I found myself right back at square one. I took on a task I wasn't meant to take because I wanted to be the agreeable good girl. Someone asked something of me, but instead of requesting time to pray, I blurted out, "Sure! I'm happy to do it." And then I felt resentful.

The same old pattern. The same old struggle. Have you been there?

Each one of us has our own battles. Some of us find ourselves lured back into the arms of drugs or alcohol after victoriously living sober. Others think we've made great progress with our spouse until we find ourselves shouting and fighting over the same old argument that has plagued us from year one.

Pornography. Binge eating. Codependency. Toxic relationships. Money management. Approval addiction. Is there anything more discouraging than finding ourselves repeating the same deadly mistakes we so valiantly worked to break free from? So we cry out to God, "Why am I here again? I thought You had healed me completely. Why can't I break free of the trap?"

I recently ran across "Autobiography in Five Short Chapters" by Portia Nelson:

CHAPTER ONE

I walk down the street.
There is a deep hole in the sidewalk.
I fall in.
I am lost. . . . I am helpless.
It isn't my fault.
It takes forever to find a way out.

CHAPTER TWO

I walk down the same street.
There is a deep hole in the sidewalk.
I pretend I don't see it.
I fall in again.

I can't believe I am in this same place.
    But, it isn't my fault.
It still takes a long time to get out.

CHAPTER THREE

I walk down the same street.
    There is a deep hole in the sidewalk.
    I see it is there.
    I still fall in . . . it's a habit . . . but,
        my eyes are open.
        I know where I am.
It is *my* fault.
I get out immediately.

CHAPTER FOUR

I walk down the same street.
    There is a deep hole in the sidewalk.
    I walk around it.

CHAPTER FIVE

I walk down another street.[14]

Godly living doesn't come naturally. We have two opposing natures inside—the flesh and the Spirit. As Paul said in Romans 7:15, he often does the very things he despises: "I do not understand what I do. For what I want to do I do not do, but what I hate I do" (NIV). Our best is fallible and frail. Yet we often think if we power through, try harder, or work smarter, we can overcome our struggles on our own. As mentioned in the poem above, we walk down a different street, thinking our problems are over, but the change is usually temporary. We avoid, but we don't go through the metamorphosis needed to be a new creature. Until we have had a heart change—a transformative rebirth—new holes and traps will appear.

LEGALISM VERSUS LOVE

If only overcoming sin and following God's will were simply a matter of willpower. How different things would be. Instead, we humans tend to waffle between an overemphasis on rules and doing whatever we want. Both choices lead to failure.

Legalism is a way of looking at the world that says, "The only thing that matters are the rules." Its focus is on obedience, which is a good thing when it comes to God's ways, but it adds more to the rule book than God intended. This is what Jesus accused the Pharisees of doing to people during his day. He gave us the definition of legalism in Matthew 23:4: "They crush people with unbearable religious demands and never lift a finger to ease the burden" (NLT). Legalism tends to come from three sources: traditions, personal opinions, and a warped view of God.

Traditions are just the way a person or group has always done things. It may or may not be based in something biblical, but it becomes so routine, so normal, that people *think* it's based on scriptural truth. It's the same for personal opinions.

We often tend to confuse personal discomfort with conviction. Whatever makes us squirm is probably not right. But just because we personally aren't comfortable with it doesn't make it wrong.

I often think of the heroes of faith from the Bible: Elijah, Mary of Bethany, Rahab, Jeremiah, Deborah, John the Baptist, Esther, and more. They were not traditional people. They wore wild clothes, had unorthodox methods, and were often perceived as abrasive or countercultural, but they were doing exactly what God told them to do. I fear if any of them walked into modern churches, they would be run out of the building.

Legalism can also be birthed by a skewed view of God. Legalists see God as a harsh taskmaster, waiting to zap and punish anyone who dares step outside His rules. The way we see God often determines our behavior.

Getting back to our personal failures, we can often have a legalistic view of our efforts. If we mess up, it's over. We've disappointed God, we've disappointed ourselves and our families. Our walk with God is a black and white set of rules and demands. The problem with this perspective is it gives no grace for being a flawed human.

Humans aren't perfect. The only perfect person to walk this earth was Jesus. If we had our act together, we would have no need of a Savior. With this mindset, we can inadvertently demand perfection from others as well. When the hurting come and offer their shattered hearts and expose their secret shames, their addictions, their struggles and scars, revealing the most vulnerable parts of themselves, more often than not they are met with a cold list of dos and don'ts. Instead of compassion, we give rules. Instead of being an accountability partner, we tell them to read their Bible more. Instead of giving them the tools they need to break free of addiction, we heap guilt on their shoulders. Why?

Lack of control births fear, and the easy way to gain control again is to create black and white rules. Follow the rules, check your list, and everything will be rosy. But no one can keep the rules. In short, legalism has never, ever healed a shattered heart.

I CAN DO IT MY WAY

On the opposite end of the spectrum, we have those who, when they fail, say, "See? Doing it God's way didn't work at all. I'm going to live life on my own terms." We may not say this overtly, but our actions imply it's what we believe.

The truth is that we all fail, so we need to shift our perspective from legalistic black-and-white thinking to realizing we eventually *will* mess up. When we accept that we can't transform on our own, we can then focus on *improvement*, not perfection.

God doesn't stand over us like a taskmaster waiting for us to stumble. He already knows that will happen. That's why He sent a Savior who yearns for connection. He longs to walk with us and teach us, whether we're scraping bottom in the valley, or soaring high on the wings of success.

HOT AIR BALLOONS

Imagine a man slowly sailing through the clouds in a bright, striped hot air balloon. The air is cool, save for the spurt of fire keeping the balloon billowy and full. As the current lifts the balloon higher and higher, the man studies the tiny images below, seeing rectangles of green and brown grass, houses, and snaking highways. Everything seems so small, and, from his vantage point, he feels so very big.

His hand cups the canvas edges of the basket wall, and he frowns. Everything is perfect except for the walls keeping him in. He wants to feel like a bird, to fly, to soar and be free. How can he do that with the ridiculous barricades in place?

He thinks to himself, *Who would create this beautiful balloon and trap its passengers in a cage underneath?* The walls were ruining his fun. Heat burned his chest at the thought. No one could tell him what to do. He was his own man.

He pulled himself over the edge and jumped, no longer bound by restrictions.

Tell me, do you think the man made a wise decision?

Some people have the mistaken idea that when you give your life to Christ, God plops a big manual in your lap filled with a list of "don'ts" and "thou shalt nots," all with the express purpose of making sure your life from then on is miserable. Not so.

Unfortunately, this is a lie even some Christians believe because they have failed to understand the true meaning of grace or are caught up in the controlling cycle of legalism.

God *does* give us boundaries to follow—a fence line, if you will, with clear warnings of what will happen if we go beyond them. He doesn't do this to ruin our life or make us miserable. God gives us boundaries to ensure we have the best life possible. Boundaries are created to keep the good things in and the bad things out.

It's no different than pulling a toddler's hand away from a hot stove or yanking a child away from an oncoming car. You tell them "no" because you don't want to see them hurt. When a child chooses to ignore a warning, they are setting themselves up for pain.

But what do children do when we tell them no? Some obey with calm submission, but many others cry, scream, kick, throw a tantrum, or even accuse their parents of being mean. Parents are no longer "good" because they aren't giving the child what they want.

Once we doubt the goodness of God, we will feel justified in rejecting His will and making our own decisions about right and wrong. And once we've shoved truth out of the picture, our life hastily spirals into a toxic mess. Bad decisions galore. And soon the opportunity to break those bad habits and choices disappears as chaos squeezes out peace.

FORBIDDEN FRUIT

Most of the time, I can't seem to get my stuff together. I have a desire to do what's good and right, but then I get distracted. I'm not settled. I can't focus. There is too much tugging at me from all directions. I forget all my good intentions when passion for my own interests captures my focus.

We are strange creatures. Oftentimes we don't want something until it's forbidden. When I'm on a diet, if I tell myself I can't have chocolate or carbs or refined sugar, that is the very thing I suddenly can't live without. The whole "forbidden fruit" mindset goes back a long way—all the way to Adam and Eve.

Adam and Eve were literally living in paradise. Perfect weather, perfect beauty, no shame or pain, delicious food, and a beautiful bond with the God who'd created them. This just proves the fallacy of the old "if-my-life-was-better-I-would-make-better-choices" argument.

God told Adam and Eve, "You are free to eat from any tree in the garden; but you must not eat from the tree of the knowledge of good and evil, for when you eat from it you will certainly die" (Genesis 2:16–17, NIV).

God basically said, "Look around you! You can do whatever you want, except eat from this tree. That's all." But Eve became fixated on the one thing she couldn't have and lost sight of the reason for the rule in the first place, that obedience is needed in order to stay connected to God. The Bible tells us, "When the woman saw that the fruit of the tree was good for food and pleasing to the eye, and also desirable for gaining wisdom, she took some and ate it. She also gave some to her husband, who was with her, and he ate it" (Genesis 3:6, NIV).

In 1 John 2:16 (NIV), the apostle John mentions the triangle of doom that wreaks havoc in our lives when we do things our own way: "For everything in the world—the lust of the flesh, the lust of the eyes, and the pride of life—comes not from the Father but from the world."

Let's take a look at each item in his list that is "not from the Father."

First, we have "the lust of the flesh." This is pleasure-seeking, whatever makes us feel good physically. Lust of the flesh says, "If it makes me feel good, it must be OK." Dangerous ground to live on.

Next, we have "the lust of the eyes." This is wanting what we see. Just because something looks good doesn't mean it is.

Finally, we have "the pride of life." This philosophy says, "It's all about me." Pride of life tells us that we are the most important thing in the world. It makes us yearn for success to puff up our own egos. It makes us crave and seek attention. We want authority, power, control, or the need to be appreciated.

In short, anything "not from the Father" will mess us up. It destroys. It shatters. It brings death, not life.

Eve embraced all three temptations. The fruit looked good, would probably taste good, and was supposed to make her wise.

Instead of the fulfillment of the good it promised, she was contaminated from the inside out and suffered misery. Trading God's best for these three is never a good swap. Never. It often leaves us in a worse condition than we were before.

Am I saying we can be sinless and perfect this side of heaven? No. But instead of relying on the lie of willpower and our own strength, the outcome is dramatically different when we partner with the Holy Spirit to explore our broken places. When we think of our lives as "perfect" or "not perfect," shame is soon to follow. Instead, we can embrace our weaknesses and view them as learning experiences, ways to relish God's grace, and see ourselves through His eyes. We need God for each day, each decision, each moment. How many of us stop and ask Him to help us when battling our own flaws and demons? How many of us want our lives to be a dance with God instead of a list of rules to be followed? I wonder if Adam and Eve's outcome would have been different if they had embraced this subtle but profound shift.

WHERE VICTORY IS FOUND

Let's return to our passage from Romans 7. Paul laments the fight between his physical body and the Spirit of God living inside him. Despite his willpower and intentions and resolutions, he fails over and over again. But Paul offers us a glimmer of hope: "Who will rescue me from this body that is subject to death? Thanks be to God, who delivers me through Jesus Christ our Lord!" (Romans 7:24–25, NIV).

What wonderful news! Despite my failures and weaknesses, God has already delivered us from the bleak future we would otherwise endure. And though we battle difficult things in this life, our eternity is secure and overflowing with joy. Although we fail, He never does. Our peace doesn't rest in our own efforts but in His.

PARTNERS

God has done for us what we could never do for ourselves, by offering us another amazing gift: the opportunity to partner with His spirit to become a better creation than we were before, shaped and molded into His very image. When we are seeking Him, He gives us the desire to be like Him—to think the way He thinks, to view the world the way He does, and to love people as an extension of His heart. The book of James tells us that God "gives us more and more grace [through the power of the Holy Spirit to defy sin and live an obedient life that reflects both our faith and our gratitude for our salvation]" (James 4:6, AMP).

God's spirit guides us in our choices, toward decisions based out of love instead of shame. And though we'll continue to stumble from time to time, He reaches down to place us back on our feet again. We don't have to strive on our own, struggling to muster willpower or figure it out through our own limited understanding. He gives us opportunity after opportunity to try again, knowing He has already placed us in the position of victory.

PETER

In the life of Peter, we have a perfect example of willpower and how it was followed by failure, shame, and restoration.

Peter was one of the Lord's most trusted disciples and friend. He was there when Jesus was transfigured (Mark 9). He saw him raise a dead girl to life (Mark 5). He witnessed countless miracles, was the first of the disciples to declare Jesus the Son of God

(Matthew 16), and was the only one willing to step out of the boat on a tumultuous sea because Jesus beckoned him to walk on water (Matthew 14).

Peter knew without a shadow of doubt that Jesus was the Messiah. He was all in. Together, they would spread Jesus's gospel. Together, they would see God's kingdom come. Together, for good or bad. Wherever Jesus went, Peter would shadow His steps. Peter's faith was unshakable, passionate, and true.

Never was this clearer than on the night Jesus was betrayed and handed over to be crucified.

> *On the way [to the Garden of Gethsemane], Jesus told them, "Tonight all of you will desert me. For the Scriptures say, 'God will strike the Shepherd, and the sheep of the flock will be scattered.' But after I have been raised from the dead, I will go ahead of you to Galilee and meet you there."*
>
> *Peter declared, "Even if everyone else deserts you, I will never desert you."*
>
> *Jesus replied, "I tell you the truth, Peter—this very night, before the rooster crows, you will deny three times that you even know me."*
>
> *"No!" Peter insisted. "Even if I have to die with you, I will never deny you!" And all the other disciples vowed the same.* Matthew 26:31–35, NLT

Peter was on fire for Jesus, so much so that he couldn't fathom what Jesus was telling him. Deny Jesus? No! Never. Not in a million years.

We need to be careful in declaring what we would never do, say, or think. That kind of hard stance reeks of self-sufficiency and doesn't consider how we all wrestle with sin. When we depend on our own abilities, at some point we will crash and burn.

We can see a chink in Peter's bravado as soon as he, the disciples, and Jesus settle in for a long night in Gethsemane.

> *Then Jesus went with them to the olive grove called Gethsemane, and he said, "Sit here while I go over there to pray." He took Peter and Zebedee's two sons, James and John, and he became anguished and distressed. He told them, "My soul is crushed with grief to the point of death. Stay here and keep watch with me."*
>
> *He went on a little farther and bowed with his face to the ground, praying, "My Father! If it is possible, let this cup of suffering be taken away from me. Yet I want your will to be done, not mine."*
>
> *Then he returned to the disciples and found them asleep. He said to Peter, "Couldn't you watch with me even one hour? Keep watch and pray, so that you will not give in to temptation. For the spirit is willing, but the body is weak!"*
> Matthew 26:36–41, NLT

Peter was given one job to do, and he fell asleep. I can so relate. In some ways, I think Peter got into trouble just because he was so zealous. Pride and passion often corrupt the best of intentions.

What Jesus said to him is the heart of the trouble with willpower. "The spirit is willing, but the body is weak!" Without seeking God continually, we can't do or be what we long to be. We are fallible creatures who make the wrong decisions.

And just as predicted, despite Peter's declarations of loyalty and love, he stumbled and fell.

> *Peter was sitting outside in the courtyard. A servant girl came over and said to him, "You were one of those with Jesus the Galilean." But Peter denied it in front of everyone.*

"I don't know what you're talking about," he said. Later, out by the gate, another servant girl noticed him and said to those standing around, "This man was with Jesus of Nazareth." Again Peter denied it, this time with an oath. "I don't even know the man," he said. A little later some of the other bystanders came over to Peter and said, "You must be one of them; we can tell by your Galilean accent." Peter swore, "A curse on me if I'm lying—I don't know the man!" And immediately the rooster crowed.

Suddenly, Jesus' words flashed through Peter's mind: "Before the rooster crows, you will deny three times that you even know me." And he went away, weeping bitterly. Matthew 26:69–75, NLT

Oh, Peter, how my heart tugs in compassion every time I read this. I get it. Despite all my convictions, my declarations, and resolutions, I have found myself in similar situations. Peter didn't believe Jesus's words but trusted in his own abilities.

One important thing to note is that Peter "wept bitterly." He wasn't just a little sad; his own panicked choice ripped his heart in two. He didn't suppress his failure by saying, "It was just one little setback. I just need more willpower." He didn't deny that it happened. "One mistake is no big deal." And he didn't feign ignorance. "Did I really resolve to do that? Doesn't sound like me." He accepted, through a torrent of weeping, what he had done, and he repented.

How many times have I believed the lie that said it was up to me—my effort, my work and my eyes on Jesus—to keep our relationship close? And while a relationship, any relationship, is a two-way street, deep in my heart I know that anything left up to my own efforts is doomed to fail.

Thankfully, when our willpower fails, grace moves in.

When we give God our broken pieces, He knits them all back together and offers a second chance, and a third, and more. When we seek Him going forward, our trips and stumbles are wrapped in His mercy and grace.

> *After breakfast Jesus asked Simon Peter, "Simon son of John, do you love me more than these?"*
>
> *"Yes, Lord," Peter replied, "you know I love you."*
>
> *"Then feed my lambs," Jesus told him. Jesus repeated the question: "Simon son of John, do you love me?"*
>
> *"Yes, Lord," Peter said, "you know I love you."*
>
> *"Then take care of my sheep," Jesus said. A third time he asked him, "Simon son of John, do you love me?"*
>
> *Peter was hurt that Jesus asked the question a third time. He said, "Lord, you know everything. You know that I love you."*
>
> *Jesus said, "Then feed my sheep."* John 21:15–17, NLT

How very like Jesus to restore Peter in such a beautiful way. Three times Peter had denied knowing Jesus, and instead, in the very location where Jesus had called him to fish for men, he gave Peter three opportunities to declare his love for him anew.

God knows the issue isn't how much we love Him, how much we've got it together, or our good intentions. He simply asks for us to bring Him what we do have, however small and weak, and allow Him to transform us into something new.

It has nothing to do with our ability and everything to do with His. What a relief.

THE BROKEN PIANO

"Great musicians should have only the finest instruments in their homes."

The caustic comment from the piano tuner who had curled up his nose at my old spinet piano has bothered me for years, though I've had a hard time figuring out why.

I thought maybe it was the man's attitude when he entered my home. I had been desperately searching for a tuner willing to take on my pawn shop find, but from the moment this guy laid eyes on it, his annoyed smirk told me the piano didn't meet his criteria. Maybe it was the chipped places around its edges. Or perhaps the slightly yellowed keys. I don't know. But before he even sat down to play it, he judged it and found it lacking.

Looking over the rim of his glasses, he shot me a scolding glare. "You are a musician, aren't you?"

"Yes, sir."

"You should be asking me to tune a baby grand, then. Or at least a piano with some kind of merit. But this . . . " He shook his head sadly. "This piano is not fit for a musician."

He then launched into a sales pitch about the wonderful pianos he had for sale in his store and grew agitated when I wouldn't bite. Needless to say, that was my one and only experience with that particular tuner.

Great musicians should have only the finest instruments in their homes. That particular comment has circled around and around in my brain for years. It bothers me. It shouldn't. That particular piano has been long gone, and I haven't seen that tuner since the day of his barbed comment yet it nags me. Why?

I finally figured out why while reading an email from a friend.

My friend detailed a wild experience she'd witnessed while attending a piano concert. A little boy somehow escaped his mother at the prestigious concert hall and crawled up on stage, plunking himself right next to a world-renowned pianist just before the man was beginning his concert. The little tyke clumsily tapped around on the keys before looking up to the famous pianist with a grin. The poor mother was horrified and jumped out of her seat, preparing to retrieve her wayward son but the pianist only smiled down at the little boy and began to imitate the toddler's finger strikes. Then something amazing happened.

As the little boy squealed with delight and pounded the keys harder, the pianist improvised melodies over the boy's tapped notes. The entire audience was spellbound. When the little boy finally tired of the game, he hopped down from the piano bench, and the musician stood and applauded him, causing the entire crowd to cheer and smile.

I love that story. And in a flash, I finally understood why that tuner's comment bothered me.

Great musicians are not great because they have the finest instruments in their homes. They aren't great because their fingers and ears are only trained for the best the world has to offer, or because they have sold a certain number of recordings, or because they fill concert halls. A real musician can make music out of any instrument. It doesn't matter whether the keys are chipped, whether it's a Bösendorfer grand or a dusty spinet, whether the action is smooth like honey or bumpy like a dirt road. It doesn't matter whether the musician is being accompanied by a great orchestra or a key-pounding little boy. The sign of a great musician is not in flaunting the world's finest instruments but the ability to make the most broken instruments sing again.

What does this analogy have to do with willpower? Our best efforts are usually an odd assortment of successes and failures. Some of us are chipped. Some are out-of-tune, and others are discouraged because we can't create the music we have tried to make in the past. We've attempted valiant efforts, but they fall short. But our own abilities don't really matter. It's about surrendering what we do have and giving it to God. He takes our broken strings, places His hands on those battered keys, and coaxes out a melody. And the more broken the instrument, the more amazing His ability to make it sing. Because, really, it's not about us. It's all about Him.

Life is a series of mistakes with a few successes thrown in. Some of us have become so paralyzed by a fear of failing, we've stopped learning. Stopped discovering. Stopped crawling outside our boxes and exploring the beauty around us. We hold onto the illusion of control, somehow thinking all will be right. No pain, no discomfort—that is, until we stumble and our world tips on its axis.

When our willpower caves in, we see our true nature. How we handle failure reveals more of our character than how we handle success. Adversity reveals the true condition of our heart. Striving for willpower is a way to pretend what's inside doesn't exist. Pressure, heat, resistance—all of it is like a hand squeezing around a toothpaste tube. It isn't until it's squeezed that we see what is truly inside. When pressure is applied, the inner person is revealed. It's easy to blame others, the system, or any other host of issues for our mistakes, but we still won't learn a thing, will we? We may even find some folks who will agree with our finger pointing, but then what? It doesn't bring us one step closer to our goals, dreams, or healing.

The only way to learn from failure is to accept it.

Some of the most beautiful things can be birthed from the messiest. God has shown it to me over and over in my own life, but it takes a heart willing to say, "I have no pride. I have no agenda. I want to learn both what to do and what not to do.

Teach me. I'm Yours." Failing doesn't feel like failure at all in that state of mind. It's just learning.

What a great place to be.

Our journeys with God are a process. They are marked with lavish grace and many mistakes. Is it frustrating when those around us keep doing the opposite of what they know to be right and good? Absolutely. But then again, it must grieve God's heart when we disobey too.

There is a story often attributed to Michelangelo that goes like this: When Michelangelo completed his statue of David, an admirer stood staring at the masterpiece in awe. The man turned to Michelangelo and asked, "However did you create such a glorious work?"

How did Michelangelo supposedly reply? "It was easy. I just chipped away the parts that didn't look like David."

That's what grace is—walking alongside God and letting Him chip away all the hard places within each of us until we resemble His Son. It isn't automatic. It doesn't come naturally, and we will face discouragement from others and ourselves. Our journeys are a cycle of failed attempts, victories, grace, and mercy.

Lysa TerKeurst calls this imperfect progress moving in the right direction. "Big things are built one brick at a time. Victories are achieved one choice at a time. A life well lived is chosen one day at a time."[15]

I'm pressing forward, imperfectly progressing toward being more and more like Jesus. The good news? I'm not alone. He is walking beside me, holding out His nail-scarred hands to veer me away from those old traps and onto new paths. But a helping hand is only beneficial if I grasp it.

BIBLE VERSE

By his divine power, God has given us everything we need for living a godly life. We have received all of this by coming to know him, the one who called us to himself by means of his marvelous glory and excellence. (2 Peter 1:3, NLT)

READER TAKEAWAY

When we rely on our own willpower, we will struggle and fail, but God asks us to give Him all of ourselves—our talents and flaws—so that He can transform us into something new. It is through His power and not our own that we can overcome our failures.

THE TRUTH

Transformation occurs when we stop relying on our own abilities and partner with God to be shaped into His image. Our goal is imperfect progress in the right direction.

QUESTION

When have you needed to rely on God's strength instead of your own willpower? What happened?

CONCLUSION
Reclaiming Our Worth

In the previous chapters, we've explored the masks of fear and how listening to them leads to bad decisions. We've examined the exhausting lie of productivity, how it demands more with each passing hour and leaves fatigue and emptiness in its wake. We've delved deep into the way we hide behind perfectionism, as well as the crippling destruction of people-pleasing. We've unearthed how depression tells us God isn't there, how insecurity hisses, "You're not good enough," and how willpower deceives us into thinking we can overcome our weaknesses on our own. All of them are heavy lies rife with consequences that can ripple throughout generations.

The good news is that we've also learned God loves us unconditionally. He is bigger than any fear and asks us to do things *with* Him instead of *for* Him. He glories in showing His strength through our weaknesses and in comforting His children when darkness attempts to shroud our souls. He died to save us because He values us so highly. He says we are more than enough through Him and offers redemption when we fail.

A line has been drawn in the sand. Lie or truth. Conviction or condemnation. Love or fear. What we think about ourselves determines how we live. The battle is for our minds. As Romans 12:2 (NLT) reminds us, "Don't copy the behavior and customs of this world, but let God transform you into a new person by changing the way you think. Then you will learn to know God's will for you, which is good and pleasing and perfect."

The world says my worth is based on how much I get done, but God says the better choice is to sit at His feet.

The world says the bigger the enemy, the more I should cower, but God says He has already slain my giants.

The world says keeping others happy will shield my heart from rejection, but God says He's already approved me.

The world says broken means worthless, but God says He delights in showing His strength through my weakness.

The world says when dark seasons occur, God has abandoned me, but God says He will never leave me or forsake me.

The world says my worth is determined by my accomplishments, but God says my worth is found in Jesus.

The world says I'll never measure up, but God declares me a masterpiece.

The world says I must be flawless to be accepted, but God says I am loved despite my flaws.

HOW TO TRANSFORM

We've discussed how these sneaky lies present themselves, and now we ask how to break free from them. After all, when we've believed something for a long time, it takes a good bit of work to undo the damage that's been done.

Here are the steps that I've found helpful in my own life:

- Recognize the lie
- Admit you fell for the deception
- Ask God for forgiveness and help
- Replace the lie with God's truth

Each step in the process is critical but none more so than *replacing* the lie with truth. Whenever we yank an old thought or habit or misbelief out of our mental repertoire, it leaves a hole inside where the lie used to reside. If we aren't quick to fill it with truth, another lie will sneak in and take up residence.

At the end of this book, I've provided a list of truths from God's Word to combat each lie we've discussed in the previous chapters. The list isn't exhaustive but is a good place to start. When those old lies try to whisper in your ear, speak God's truth aloud. Scribble truths on sticky notes and leave them scattered around the house or car. Put reminders in your phone. Saturate your mind and heart with what God says about you. You are who He says you are. God is the only One who never changes. He is our security. If we can wrap His truth around our minds and let it soak into our marrow, it will change everything about the way we live and choose and grow and develop. Truth is transformational. Truth is freedom.

RECLAIMING OUR WORTH

To reclaim something means to take back what once was ours. It carries with it the idea of taking something that was debased and restoring it to its former glory. Lies destroy and tarnish. They corrode the way we see God and ourselves. Kicking those deceptions to the curb is to snatch back the confidence we once walked with.

My middle daughter is a fantastic swimmer. She's won multiple awards and had the opportunity to compete in the junior Olympics but was waylaid by a shoulder injury.

Although she loved swimming, one thing she didn't particularly enjoy was the long arduous work of a swim meet. There is a lot of downtime. Numbers are continually being mumbled over loudspeakers. The angst of competition, the stress of beating your best score—all while standing around in a dripping bathing suit half the day, desperately trying to keep your muscles warmed up while being forced to sit and wait. The meets can be miserable at times.

At one particular swim meet, I could tell Callie wasn't feeling it. Her asthma had been acting up, and the school week had been more demanding than usual. She sighed, slinging her backpack onto the unforgiving bench to wait, until she heard some girls nearby talking about her. Their not-so-quiet whispers drifted through the muggy natatorium air.

"See her? Yeah, the blond girl. She's really good. Tough to beat. I hope I don't have to compete in the same heat as her."

My daughter suddenly exuded a new confidence. She lifted her chin and pulled her shoulders back. Nothing had really changed, but being reminded who she was changed her perspective. In other words, she began to walk *from* a position of victory instead of trying to *achieve* victory. And that, my friend, is what God wants for each of us. He yearns to lovingly craft us into the creation He intended us to be before we fell for the lies.

THE INVITATION

Lies restrict our freedom and bind us to our failures. They tie us to our mistakes and make us think the pain of today will carry into tomorrow. They might have formed us into the person we are today, but our present doesn't have to become our future.

It's time to identify the lies we believed about ourselves and nail them to Jesus's cross.

In a beautiful plea, Jennifer Dukes Lee states, "Christ continually shouts through the universe, 'You have a love that is already yours. You have nothing to prove to anyone. You have nothing to prove to Me. You are significant and preapproved and utterly cherished. Not because you are "good," but because you are Mine.'"[16]

He saw you before He laid the foundation of the world. When He breathed life into the lungs of man, He loved you. When He wove you cell by cell inside your mother's womb, He rejoiced over you. And when He hung on a cruel cross, suspended between Heaven and earth, He thought of you. He wants more for you than any lie could ever provide.

He offers each of us an invitation. An opportunity to break free from the lies. For Him, it's never been about our performance, how badly we've messed up or how worthy we feel. He offers us the opportunity to come to Him with all of our broken pieces and lay them down.

We have been invited to learn and play and create and cry and laugh with the God of the universe. He wants us to know Him.

And in knowing God, we'll come to understand who we truly are.

BIBLE VERSE

It is for freedom that Christ has set us free. Stand firm, then, and do not let yourselves be burdened again by a yoke of slavery. (Galatians 5:1, NIV)

READER TAKEAWAY

It is possible to find freedom from our pasts, our failures, and the lies we believe about ourselves, but we have to identify the lie, admit that we've fallen for it, and then replace the lie with God's truth. This shift forges a new way of thinking and prioritizes our walk with Him in order to find rest and peace.

THE TRUTH

When we realize how deeply we are loved by the God of the universe, how deep His mercy and unfathomable His grace, we can let go of the lies, the fears, and our old habits and ways of living.

QUESTION

What have you learned? Write out a prayer to God, thanking Him for His love and asking Him to transform your life from the inside out.

APPENDIX

Finding Truth in God's Word

THE LIE OF FEAR

Affirmation: "God will help me."

> *"Don't be afraid, for I am with you. Don't be discouraged, for I am your God. I will strengthen you and help you. I will hold you up with my victorious right hand."* Isaiah 41:10, NLT

> *Fearing people is a dangerous trap, but trusting the LORD means safety.* Proverbs 29:25, NLT

Affirmation: "Fear and love cannot coexist; so if I'm fearful, I'm not leaning into love."

> *For God has not given us a spirit of fear and timidity, but of power, love, and self-discipline.* 2 Timothy 1:7, NLT

> *Such love has no fear, because perfect love expels all fear. If we are afraid, it is for fear of punishment, and this shows that we have not fully experienced his perfect love.* 1 John 4:18, NLT

Affirmation: “God will deliver me.”

I prayed to the LORD, and he answered me. He freed me from all my fears. Psalm 34:4, NLT

Affirmation: “God is with me and will protect me.”

“This is my command—be strong and courageous! Do not be afraid or discouraged. For the LORD your God is with you wherever you go.” Joshua 1:9, NLT

“Be sure of this: I am with you always, even to the end of the age.” Matthew 28:20, NLT

He will cover you with his feathers. He will shelter you with his wings. His faithful promises are your armor and protection. Psalm 91:4, NLT

“I give them eternal life, and they will never perish. No one can snatch them away from me, for my Father has given them to me, and he is more powerful than anyone else. No one can snatch them from the Father’s hand.” John 10:28–29, NLT

THE LIE OF PRODUCTIVITY

Affirmation: “It’s OK to rest.”

“Be still, and know that I am God!” Psalm 46:10, NLT

“The LORD himself will fight for you. Just stay calm.” Exodus 14:14, NLT

Jesus said, “Come to me, all of you who are weary and carry heavy burdens, and I will give you rest. Take my yoke

upon you. Let me teach you, because I am humble and gentle at heart, and you will find rest for your souls. For my yoke is easy to bear, and the burden I give you is light." Matthew 11:28–30, NLT

Affirmation: "I don't have to worry and be anxious about getting everything done."

Don't worry about anything; instead, pray about everything. Tell God what you need, and thank him for all he has done. Then you will experience God's peace, which exceeds anything we can understand. His peace will guard your hearts and minds as you live in Christ Jesus. Philippians 4:6–7, NLT

Whether you eat or drink, or whatever you do, do it all for the glory of God. 1 Corinthians 10:31, NLT

Affirmation: "True success is found in Jesus, not finishing my checklist."

They delight in the law of the LORD, meditating on it day and night. They are like trees planted along the riverbank, bearing fruit each season. Their leaves never wither, and they prosper in all they do. Psalm 1:2–3, NLT

THE LIE OF PERFECTIONISM

Affirmation: "God can use me just as I am."

He said, "My grace is all you need. My power works best in weakness." So now I am glad to boast about my weaknesses, so that the power of Christ can work through me. 2 Corinthians 12:9, NLT

When I first came to you, dear brothers and sisters, I didn't use lofty words and impressive wisdom to tell you God's secret plan. For I decided that while I was with you I would forget everything except Jesus Christ, the one who was crucified. I came to you in weakness—timid and trembling. And my message and my preaching were very plain. Rather than using clever and persuasive speeches, I relied only on the power of the Holy Spirit. I did this so you would trust not in human wisdom but in the power of God. 1 Corinthians 2:1–5, NLT

Affirmation: "When my focus is on Jesus, I am complete."

The Lord said to her, "My dear Martha, you are worried and upset over all these details! There is only one thing worth being concerned about. Mary has discovered it, and it will not be taken away from her." Luke 10:41–42, NLT

For by that one offering he forever made perfect those who are being made holy. Hebrews 10:14, NLT

THE LIE OF PEOPLE-PLEASING

Affirmation: "I cannot be God's servant if I'm obsessed with pleasing people."

Obviously, I'm not trying to win the approval of people, but of God. If pleasing people were my goal, I would not be Christ's servant. Galatians 1:10, NLT

Work willingly at whatever you do, as though you were working for the Lord rather than for people. Colossians 3:23, NLT

Our purpose is to please God, not people. He alone examines the motives of our hearts. 1 Thessalonians 2:4, NLT

Don't you realize that friendship with the world makes you an enemy of God? I say it again: If you want to be a friend of the world, you make yourself an enemy of God. James 4:4, NLT

Affirmation: "God has already approved me."

The LORD is for me, so I will have no fear. What can mere people do to me? Yes, the LORD is for me; he will help me. I will look in triumph at those who hate me. It is better to take refuge in the LORD than to trust in people. It is better to take refuge in the LORD than to trust in princes. Psalm 118:6–9, NLT

When people commend themselves, it doesn't count for much. The important thing is for the Lord to commend them. 2 Corinthians 10:18, NLT

For whoever finds me finds life and receives favor from the LORD. Proverbs 8:35, NLT

THE LIE OF DEPRESSION

Affirmation: "God sees me."

"Can anyone hide from me in a secret place? Am I not everywhere in all the heavens and earth?" says the LORD. Jeremiah 23:24, NLT

Thereafter, Hagar used another name to refer to the LORD, who had spoken to her. She said, "You are the God who sees me." Genesis 16:13, NLT

Affirmation: "God cares about me."

The LORD hears his people when they call to him for help. He rescues them from all their troubles. The LORD is close to the brokenhearted; he rescues those whose spirits are crushed. Psalm 34:17–18, NLT

Give all your worries and cares to God, for he cares about you. 1 Peter 5:7, NLT

Even though I walk through the darkest valley, I will fear no evil, for you are with me; your rod and your staff, they comfort me. Psalm 23:4, NIV

Affirmation: "Suffering doesn't last forever."

In his kindness God called you to share in his eternal glory by means of Christ Jesus. So after you have suffered a little while, he will restore, support, and strengthen you, and he will place you on a firm foundation. 1 Peter 5:10, NLT

Affirmation: "I can find healing."

O LORD, if you heal me, I will be truly healed; if you save me, I will be truly saved. My praises are for you alone! Jeremiah 17:14, NLT

You, O LORD, are a shield around me; you are my glory, the one who holds my head high. Psalm 3:3, NLT

THE LIE OF INSECURITY

Affirmation: "God made me for a purpose."

Thank you for making me so wonderfully complex! Your workmanship is marvelous—how well I know it. Psalm 139:14, NLT

For we are His workmanship, created in Christ Jesus for good works, which God prepared beforehand, that we should walk in them. Ephesians 2:10, NKJV

Affirmation: "God loves me."

I am convinced that nothing can ever separate us from God's love. Neither death nor life, neither angels nor demons, neither our fears for today nor our worries about tomorrow—not even the powers of hell can separate us from God's love. Romans 8:38, NLT

Affirmation: "There is no need to compare myself to anyone."

Pay careful attention to your own work, for then you will get the satisfaction of a job well done, and you won't need to compare yourself to anyone else. Galatians 6:4, NLT

A peaceful heart leads to a healthy body; jealousy is like cancer in the bones. Proverbs 14:30, NLT

THE LIE OF WILLPOWER

Affirmation: "Despite my best efforts, I will fail from time to time."

Indeed, we all make many mistakes. For if we could control our tongues, we would be perfect and could also control ourselves in every other way. James 3:2, NLT

Everyone has sinned; we all fall short of God's glorious standard. Romans 3:23, NLT

Let me ask you this one question: Did you receive the Holy Spirit by obeying the law of Moses? Of course not! You received the Spirit because you believed the message you heard about Christ. How foolish can you be?

> *After starting your new lives in the Spirit, why are you now trying to become perfect by your own human effort?* Galatians 3:2–3, NLT

Affirmation: "The Holy Spirit works with me to overcome what I can't do on my own."

> *The Holy Spirit helps us in our weakness. For example, we don't know what God wants us to pray for. But the Holy Spirit prays for us with groanings that cannot be expressed in words.* Romans 8:26, NLT

> *Therefore he is able, once and forever, to save those who come to God through him. He lives forever to intercede with God on their behalf.* Hebrews 7:25, NLT

> *By his divine power, God has given us everything we need for living a godly life. We have received all of this by coming to know him, the one who called us to himself by means of his marvelous glory and excellence.* 2 Peter 1:3, NLT

> *No, despite all these things, overwhelming victory is ours through Christ, who loved us.* Romans 8:37, NLT

> *The Spirit of God, who raised Jesus from the dead, lives in you.* Romans 8:11, NLT

Affirmation: "I am not condemned."

> *Now there is no condemnation for those who belong to Christ Jesus. And because you belong to him, the power of the life-giving Spirit has freed you from the power of sin that leads to death.* Romans 8:1–2, NLT

> *I am writing to you who are God's children because your sins have been forgiven through Jesus.* 1 John 2:12, NLT

TRUTHS ABOUT YOUR WORTH

Affirmation: "I am loved by God."

"I knew you before I formed you in your mother's womb." Jeremiah 1:5, NLT

O Lord, you have examined my heart and know everything about me. You know when I sit down or stand up. You know my thoughts even when I'm far away. You see me when I travel and when I rest at home. You know everything I do. You know what I am going to say even before I say it, Lord. You go before me and follow me. You place your hand of blessing on my head. Such knowledge is too wonderful for me, too great for me to understand! Psalm 139:1–6, NLT

Affirmation: "I am God's heir."

Now you are no longer a slave but God's own child. And since you are his child, God has made you his heir. Galatians 4:7, NLT

Affirmation: "I am chosen."

We know, dear brothers and sisters, that God loves you and has chosen you to be his own people. 1 Thessalonians 1:4, NLT

Affirmation: "I am a new creation."

This means that anyone who belongs to Christ has become a new person. The old life is gone; a new life has begun! 2 Corinthians 5:17, NLT

Affirmation: "I am God's child."

See how very much our Father loves us, for he calls us his children, and that is what we are! But the people who belong

> *to this world don't recognize that we are God's children because they don't know him.* 1 John 3:1, NLT

Affirmation: "I am God's temple."

> *Don't you realize that all of you together are the temple of God and that the Spirit of God lives in you?* 1 Corinthians 3:16, NLT

Affirmation: "My future is in heaven."

> *We are citizens of heaven, where the Lord Jesus Christ lives. And we are eagerly waiting for him to return as our Savior.* Philippians 3:20, NLT

> *"For this is how God loved the world: He gave his one and only Son, so that everyone who believes in him will not perish but have eternal life."* John 3:16, NLT

> *"Don't let your hearts be troubled. Trust in God, and trust also in me. There is more than enough room in my Father's home. If this were not so, would I have told you that I am going to prepare a place for you? When everything is ready, I will come and get you, so that you will always be with me where I am."* John 14:1–3, NLT

Small-Group Guide

Welcome to the study guide for *The Lies That Bind*. Whether you've led countless study groups or this is your first, this guide is meant to help you through the uncertainty and challenges that come with leading a group of people into understanding how deeply they are loved by God. You are a beautiful part of His plan.

Group meetings for this study are usually best utilized when aiming for a meeting of an hour or less. Since some of the topics in this book can be weighty, it's best to start with a light tone and warm introductions. As detailed below, a three-prong meeting usually works well.

First part: Open with prayer, make introductions or announcements, and review what was discussed or learned the previous week.

Second part: Read the opening of the chapter, using video links where appropriate, and give time for participants to respond. Identify the lie that is being discussed and cover the questions listed in this small-group guide. Encourage everyone to ask questions, share, respond, or read along. Because some of these topics require a high degree of vulnerability, it is important not to force anyone to share if they aren't ready. Silence is not bad if participants are thinking and processing, but one person should not dominate the conversation. Book studies like this work best when there is a lot of sharing. The shy attendees are more likely to participate if they feel heard, comfortable, and safe. Along these lines, it is a good idea to remind the participants that what is said in the small group should remain there. The goal is to draw closer to Christ and to one another. You do not need to have all the answers. Your contribution is to keep conversation flowing and direct the attendees back to the truth in God's Word.

Third part: Return to the truth of what/who God says we are. God's Word is the central focus of each chapter. Continually point participants to the truth so less attention is given to the lie. This is the point where healing can begin. Close with questions, encouragement, and prayer.

Bonus: Some groups enjoy trying a memory verse challenge each week. Think of fun ways to reward one another for memorizing them. Another option is to write the memory verse on Post-its and stick them to vital places in each attendee's environment, like the car, the kitchen, the bathroom mirrors, etc.

Connection after each meeting is extremely beneficial. Some ways to do this are by using a sharing connection/announcements app like Band, GroupMe, or the like. Sharing funny videos related to upcoming content, etc., can be helpful, as are Bible verses, offering space for prayer requests or weekly wins.

I would also encourage doing something extra special to conclude the end of the study, whether that's a shared meal, celebration, or other get-together.

INTRODUCTION: THE LIE ABOUT ME

READER TAKEAWAY

At one time or another, we have all fallen for a lie, and believing that lie will leave us stuck in an exhausting cycle.

Most of us have had dark moments in our lives, like the one described in the opening of this book. List three of your life's highlights and three of your dark moments. Pick one of those moments and relive the emotion that washed over you during that time. List a few emotions that come to mind.

High #1:

High #2:

High #3:

Low #1:

Low #2:

Low #3:

Emotions experienced:

Because of that dark moment in the bathroom, I'm not a huge fan of bath mats. What is something that most people love that you do not because of an emotional connotation connected to it?

Recall some of the negative comments I've heard from women around the country. Put a checkmark next to the ones you've thought about yourself.

- ☐ *"No one could ever love me if they knew the real me."*
- ☐ *"If I feel something, it must be true."*
- ☐ *"I don't have value."*
- ☐ *"God couldn't love me after what I've done."*
- ☐ *"I'm a horrible wife/mom/daughter/friend."*
- ☐ *"My past will always destroy my future."*
- ☐ *"God is against me."*
- ☐ *"If my circumstances were different, I would be different."*

Is there another negative thought you've had about yourself? How often does it appear? What is your usual response?

....

....

....

Recall an import passage from the introduction:

> Sometimes, our misbeliefs feel identical to truth. They feel right because at one moment in our life someone or some event reinforced them. As we grow up, those misbeliefs are clues we receive that tell us how the world seems to work. They shape our worldview and become the filter through which we see everything.

What do you picture when you hear the words *barking dog*?

....

....

....

Why do you think there were different answers among the group members?

....

....

....

Do you agree with the statement: *We know that lies hurt us, but they are especially destructive when we believe them.* Why or why not?

....

....

....

Your current ______________________ don't have to become your ______________________.

BIBLE VERSE CHALLENGE

Dear friends, do not believe every spirit, but test the spirits to see whether they are from God. (1 John 4:1, NIV)

CHAPTER 1: THE LIE OF FEAR

READER TAKEAWAY

If any of us is struggling with feeling our life is no longer joyful, then it may be because we are living with some form of unidentified fear.

The wind and the waves don't obey ________ ________, but they do obey the voice of ________________.

FEAR can be thought of as

____

What are some masks fear has used in your own life? How long did it take you to realize what you were actually feeling was fear?

....

....

....

What are ways we can feed love instead of fear?

....

....

....

What is the difference between fear and clinical anxiety?

....

....

....

When kids are scared, where is the first place they run? Into the arms of their parents. We're the same way. When something is too hard, too complex, too overwhelming for us to understand, we have a need for God. Not only does He hold us when we're afraid, but He's given us tools as well.

- Prayer: We can pray for guidance and to feel God's presence.
- Perspective: We can measure the size of our fear against the size of God.
- Praise: We can praise Him even in the midst of our worry.

What is your greatest fear? How could you turn this fear over to God?

BIBLE VERSE CHALLENGE

There is no fear in love. But perfect love drives out fear, because fear has to do with punishment. The one who fears is not made perfect in love. (1 John 4:18, NLT)

CHAPTER 2: THE LIE OF PRODUCTIVITY

READER TAKEAWAY

Working *for* God is not the same as being close *to* God. Productivity leads to exhaustion, but when we find our worth in our relationship with Jesus, we can rest.

What are some things you do that might be considered "toxic productivity"?

Are you more like Mary or Martha? Why?

Take a moment to create a to-do list for the coming week. Then create a to-be list.

To Do

____

____

____

To Be

____

____

____

Put a star next to the items that are the most important to you. Why are they important?

God is more interested in ____________ than He is in us doing things ____________ Him.

Have you ever struggled with physical, emotional, or spiritual burnout? What do you believe caused it?

BIBLE VERSE CHALLENGE

"For I desire mercy, not sacrifice, and acknowledgment of God rather than burnt offerings." (Hosea 6:6, NIV)

CHAPTER 3: THE LIE OF PERFECTIONISM

READER TAKEAWAY

Hiding behind a mask of perfectionism always fails at some point. Just as we see in the art of *kintsugi*, there is great beauty in imperfection and brokenness.

Did you have a favorite princess or character you identified with in childhood? Did this admiration cause you to have unrealistic expectations as you grew into adulthood?

Why do you think so many of us hide who we truly are?

Name some things that are better when they are broken:

What do you use as your spiritual "makeup" to hide?

In what ways does our culture try to convince us "perfect" is real?

List your greatest achievement.

Now add, "and Jesus loves me unconditionally" after it.

List your greatest failure.

Now add "and Jesus loves me unconditionally" after it.

BIBLE VERSE CHALLENGE

"First clean the inside of the cup and dish, and then the outside also will be clean." (Matthew 23:26, NIV)

CHAPTER 4: THE LIE OF PEOPLE-PLEASING

READER TAKEAWAY

Living a life of people-pleasing in the name of doing things for God cannot be sustained. Eventually our masks will crumble, but God is gracious to reveal our true motives with gentleness and love.

What is the weirdest thing you've lied about in order to fit in?

....

....

....

Check the items that you experience often. How many did you score out of 13? ___________

- ☐ *You find it nearly impossible to say "no" to a request.*
- ☐ *You sometimes feel responsible for the mood of others.*
- ☐ *You tell people what they want to hear to avoid conflict.*
- ☐ *You feel like it is your responsibility to keep others happy.*
- ☐ *You often find yourself responsible for tasks that you really don't want to do.*
- ☐ *You feel uneasy about the decisions you've made until you receive approval from others.*
- ☐ *You bend over backwards to get people to like you, even if you don't really like them.*
- ☐ *When having to say "no" to a request, you feel the need to explain the reason why.*
- ☐ *You keep your opinions to yourself because you fear rejection.*
- ☐ *You apologize excessively or often.*
- ☐ *You feel resentment toward people who make requests of your time and/or talent.*

- ☐ *After being at a party or other social event, you replay conversations you had with others over and over in your mind.*
- ☐ *You constantly worry that something you said might have offended someone.*

When I was little and in Sunday School, I was taught a song titled "O-B-E-D-I-E-N-C-E." It used to drive my dad crazy because my brother and I would sing it at the top of our lungs while doing things that we knew we weren't supposed to— primarily, sliding down the stairs on the couch cushions. Dad would shake his head. "Somehow, I think you two are missing the point of the song!"

What songs/ideas were you taught as a child that could have inadvertently caused you to focus on the performance side of obeying versus the motivation?

....

....

....

What does the word *ministry* mean to you?

....

....

....

How is this different than people-pleasing?

____________________ and ______________________ are not the same thing.

BIBLE VERSE CHALLENGE

Am I now trying to win the approval of human beings, or of God? Or am I trying to please people? If I were still trying to please people, I would not be a servant of Christ. (Galatians 1:10, NIV)

CHAPTER 5: THE LIE OF DEPRESSION

READER TAKEAWAY

Depression is a lie that tells us God either isn't with us or doesn't care about our suffering. If we believe these lies, we will be left despondent and doubting God's goodness.

What are some ways our emotions lie to us?

Can you think of other people in the Bible who battled depression, like David and Elijah?

If you are currently battling depression, here are some things that might help.

1. **Seek medical attention.** Depression may result from a chemical imbalance. It takes an extremely long time for these chemicals to replenish, if at all. It just depends on the person and the reason. Medication will help give you relief from the symptoms while you work to explore the cause.
2. **Seek counseling with a trusted Christian counselor.** It is incredibly important that the person trying to help you dig to the core of who you are is a follower of Christ. It is God who ultimately does the revealing and healing.

3. **Listen to upbeat praise and worship music.** Whether classic hymns or contemporary songs, listening to music can help reduce anxiety and stress.
4. **Pray.** Even if it is hard to form the words to pray, cry out to God. He hears you, even if He seems far away.
5. **Share with someone you trust.** But make sure the person is "safe." A safe person is one who will not immediately condemn you. This is a person who will listen, be there for you, and speak the truth in love. Confiding in an unsafe person will only deepen your feelings of hopelessness.
6. **If you can, read your Bible.** This is often hard for some people in the middle of this storm. I had a friend who battled this and she was physically unable to read. Her eyes blurred and she couldn't concentrate on a single sentence. That's OK. You can go to www.biblegateway.com and listen to free audio versions.
7. **Make small goals.** Some people have functional depression. They can get up, go to work, take care of their kids, but collapse into bed later. Some are completely unable to rise from bed. In this scenario, it's especially important to take your recovery slow but steady. For starters, make a victory journal. Jot down any progress. Even if you are only able to rise out of bed for thirty minutes and move to a different room, that is a victory! Write it down. Work a puzzle. Do a load of laundry. Go to a movie. These may seem small, but they are monumental in helping you reclaim the life God intended you to have.

HALT!

HALT is a great way to remember to take care of yourself. HALT reminds us not to let ourselves get hungry, angry, lonely, or tired. If you leave yourself vulnerable to these things, it's a very quick spiral down again.

With depression, you cannot operate based on how you ________________. You have to cling to what you ______________.

BIBLE VERSE CHALLENGE

Even when I walk through the darkest valley, I will not be afraid, for you are close beside me. Your rod and your staff protect and comfort me. (Psalm 23:4, NLT)

CHAPTER 6: THE LIE OF INSECURITY

READER TAKEAWAY

Insecurity is a result of not embracing our worth in Christ and hiding our wounds from the One who can heal them. A sure sign of its presence is jealousy, and it can cause us to live a life of condemning emotions and behaviors.

If you were a house, what would it look like?

....

....

....

A sure sign of insecurity is ____________________________________.

Why do you think we compare ourselves to others?

....

....

....

Do you have a nickname? If so, what is it? Does it uplift you or demean your perceived worth?

....

....

....

Write a God-worth statement about yourself.

....

....

....

Write this statement on a Post-it note and stick it various places around your house, work, or car: ***My worth is not measured by what I do or how I look but by what He has done for me.***

How would your life be different if you were able to lay down your insecurity?

....

....

....

BIBLE VERSE CHALLENGE

There is no condemnation for those who belong to Christ Jesus. (Romans 8:1, NLT)

CHAPTER 7: THE LIE OF WILLPOWER

READER TAKEAWAY

When we rely on our own willpower, we will struggle and fail, but God asks us to give Him all of ourselves—our talents and flaws—so that He can transform us into something new. It is through His power and not our own that we can overcome our failures.

Take a few moments and watch the "Stop It!" sketch with Bob Newhart.

What is something you've struggled with overcoming? Why do you think you have trouble breaking this habit?

Has someone ever told you to "just stop" a destructive habit? Did it work? Why or why not?

What are some "hard places" God may be trying to chip away from you so you more closely resemble His Son?

The Bible is full of people like Peter who tried to do the right thing but failed. Who are some other Biblical examples you relate to in this regard? What can you learn from their choices and how God responded?

The goal is ____________________ ____________________ in the right direction. Messing up is certain. That is why God sent us a Savior.

BIBLE VERSE CHALLENGE

By his divine power, God has given us everything we need for living a godly life. We have received all of this by coming to know him, the one who called us to himself by means of his marvelous glory and excellence. (2 Peter 1:3, NLT)

CONCLUSION: RECLAIMING OUR WORTH

READER TAKEAWAY

It is possible to find freedom from our pasts, our failures, and the lies we believed about ourselves, but we have to identify the lie, admit that we've fallen for it, and then replace the lie with God's truth. This shift forges a new way of thinking, and prioritizes our walk with Him in order to find rest and peace.

The battle is for our ____________________________.

List the four steps needed to kick lies to the curb.

1.
2.
3.
4.

Is rest easy for you or hard?

How can you build "Sabbath rest" into your weekly schedule?

....

....

....

"Sometimes I'm busy learning __________ God, but I'm not connecting __________ God. I'm doing things __________ God, but I'm not spending time __________ Him.

How do you view God? How do you think He sees you?

....

....

....

What have you learned? Write out a prayer to God, thanking Him for His love and asking Him to transform your life from the inside out.

....

....

....

BIBLE VERSE CHALLENGE

It is for freedom that Christ has set us free. Stand firm, then, and do not let yourselves be burdened again by a yoke of slavery. (Galatians 5:1, NIV)

Notes

1. Jennifer Dukes Lee, *Love Idol: Letting Go of Your Need for Approval and Seeing Yourself through God's Eyes* (Tyndale House Publishers, Inc., 2014), 118.
2. Shauna Niequist, *Present Over Perfect: Leaving Behind Frantic for a Simpler, More Soulful Way of Living* (Zondervan, 2016), 24.
3. Briana LaGrow, *A Tale of Two Wolves: A Native American Legend About the Power of Choice* (Self-published, 2023).
4. *Cool Runnings*, directed by Jon Turteltaub (1993; Buena Vista Pictures Distribution).
5. Vance Havner, "The Use of Broken Things," in *Illustrations Unlimited: A Topical Collection of Hundreds of Stories, Quotations & Humor for Speakers, Writers, Pastors and Teachers*, ed. James D. Hewett (Tyndale House Publishers, Inc., 1988), 15.
6. Bob Goff, *Love Does: Discover a Secretly Incredible Life in an Ordinary World* (Thomas Nelson, 2012), 57. https://www.goodreads.com/quotes/1171538-it-has-always-seemed-to-me-that-broken-things-just.
7. Brené Brown, *Rising Strong: How the Ability to Reset Transforms the Way We Live, Love, Parent, and Lead* (Random House, 2017), 4.

8. Santiago Delboy, "The Dilemma of the People-Pleasing Chameleon," *Psychology Today*, April 9, 2025. https://www.psychologytoday.com/us/blog/relationships-healing-relationships/202503/the-dilemma-of-the-people-pleasing-chameleon.
9. C. H. Spurgeon, *The Metropolitan Tabernacle Pulpit: Sermons* (London: Passmore & Alabaster, 1834–1892), vol. 36, 200.
10. C. H. Spurgeon, *The Metropolitan Tabernacle Pulpit: Sermons* (London: Passmore & Alabaster, 1834–1892), vol. 23, 270.
11. Dawn Daniels, "'The Cracked Pot'—A folktale from India–adapted by Dawn Daniels," UUFCM Sermons by Dawn Daniels (blog), March 5, 2017. https://www.uufcm.org/uploads/1/4/9/0/14901058/170305storythecrackedpot.pdf.
12. Chuck Swindoll, "Holding on Loosely," *Insight for Living*, April 11, 2013. https://www.insight.org/resources/article-library/individual/holding-on-loosely.
13. *Mad TV*, season 6, episode 24, "New Therapy," featuring Bob Newhart and Mo Collins, aired May 12, 2001. https://www.youtube.com/watch?v=aAhA7KfbJgg&t=7s.
14. Portia Nelson, "Autobiography in Five Short Chapters," in *There's a Hole in My Sidewalk: The Romance of Self-Discovery* (Atria Paperback/Beyond Words, 2018), xi–xii.
15. Lysa TerKeurst, *Made to Crave Devotional: 60 Days to Craving God, Not Food* (Zondervan, 2011), 90.
16. Jennifer Dukes Lee, *Love Idol: Letting Go of Your Need for Approval and Seeing Yourself through God's Eyes* (Tyndale House Publishers, Inc., 2014), 171.

Acknowledgments

Every attempt has been made to credit the sources of copyrighted material used in this book. If any such acknowledgment has been inadvertently omitted or miscredited, receipt of such information would be appreciated.

A Note from the Editors

We hope you enjoyed *The Lies That Bind,* published by Guideposts. For over 75 years, Guideposts, a nonprofit organization, has been driven by a vision of a world filled with hope. We aspire to be the voice of a trusted friend, a friend who makes you feel more hopeful and connected.

By making a purchase from Guideposts, you join our community in touching millions of lives, inspiring them to believe that all things are possible through faith, hope, and prayer. Your continued support allows us to provide uplifting resources to those in need. Whether through our communities, websites, apps, or publications, we inspire our audiences, bring them together, and comfort, uplift, entertain, and guide them. Visit us at guideposts.org to learn more.

We would love to hear from you. Write us at Guideposts, P.O. Box 5815, Harlan, Iowa 51593 or call us at (800) 932-2145. Did you love *The Lies That Bind*? Leave a review for this product on guideposts.org/shop. Your feedback helps others in our community find relevant products.